Traditional Pubs

of Old Lancashire

including Manchester
& Liverpool

Peter Barnes

Wilmslow, England

Published by Sigma Leisure – an imprint of
Sigma Press, 1 South Oak Lane, Wilmslow, Cheshire, SK9 6AR, England.

Whilst every effort has been made to ensure that the information given in this book is correct, neither the publisher nor the author accept any responsibility for any inaccuracy nor for any injury, howsoever caused.

PPR

British Library Cataloguing in Publication Data
A CIP record for this book is available from the British Library.

05427515

ISBN: 1-85058-296-3

Typesetting and Design by: Sigma Press, Wilmslow, Cheshire.

Maps by: Peter Cash

Text photographs by: the author, except for those on pages 106, 109, and 113, taken by Claire Hunt.

Cover Design by: Martin G. Mills

Printed and bound by: Manchester Free Press, Paragon Mill, Jersey St., Manchester M4 6FP.

Foreword

One of the ironies of an age which recognises the value of heritage and tradition is that, very often, we do not appreciate what we have until we have lost it. Twenty years ago CAMRA saw that danger in our wide range of traditional beers and has fought strenuously since to retain the best of what we have. One of the ways in which this was done was by means of beer guides which brought the quality and variety of our indigenous ales to a wider audience.

CAMRA recognises that the traditional pub is also an institution which is an integral part of our national heritage and must be conserved wherever possible. Indeed, this is more critical than the retention of traditional ales, because real ales can be re-introduced, whereas a demolished or radically altered pub is lost forever.

Once again, the documentation of our existing pubs is an important strand of a strategy to retain and conserve pubs of character. By making these pubs accessible to a wider audience their value will be more appreciated and, perhaps, their slow demise may be arrested. Peter Barnes' compendium of Lancashire's traditional pubs demonstrates the variety of premises which we still posess. Peter's enthusiasm for his subject shines through and will, I feel, prove contagious and encourage customers, licensees and brewers alike to take a fresh look at what they have and how they may best ensure its survival, other than in museums and heritage parks.

Roger Hall,

CAMRA Pub Preservation Officer – Greater Manchester

Acknowledgements

Pauline, my wife, for patience and assistance.

Tony Buller, John Clarke, Geoff Johnson and Sean Murphy for advice and some helpful suggestions on where to find worthy pubs.

Claire Hunt for the use of her MA dissertation "The Public House in Greater Manchester: A Subject for Conservation", and for photographs.

Various Neil Richardson publications - a series of booklets by different authors on the history of pubs in the Manchester area and a valuable source of historical data.

Manchester City Council for permission to use a sketch of Sinclair's Oyster Bar.

Whitbread plc and Whitbread Archive Collection for permission to use illustrations on pages 1 and 2 from *'Word for Word: an Encyclopædia of Beer'*

'Opening Times' magazine for permission to use a map.

Peter Barnes

Disclaimer:

Every effort has been made to ensure the accuracy of the information in this guide but no responsibility can be accepted for errors. Recent Government legislation is resulting in many changes in pub ownership and tenure. Consequently, there are changes in the way the pubs are run. However, successful pubs, like the ones listed here, should be less vulnerable than others.

Contents

"The public house represents what should be the hub of our wheel of life, essential to our material need and second only to the Church that stands and represents our spiritual necessity. The Church is to the spirit as the inn is to the flesh, and, if good and well designed, they baulk the devil himself".

Edwin Lutyens, quoted in *The Builder,* October 15th, 1937

Good wholesome BEER

EVERY MAN WORTH HIS SALT likes a good glass of beer. When you've worked hard or played hard the very sight of a freshly-drawn pint puts new life in you. It's such a grand invigorating drink. Call in at The Local next time you need a refresher—you'll find good company as well as good beer. And your wife will enjoy it too. She may go for light or brown ale, or a stout. There's a beer to suit every taste—and, draught or bottled, it's the best long drink in the world!

The best long drink in the world!

Traditional Pubs

It is hard to spot a good pub. Some of the best ones are to be found in the most unlikely places and sometimes a pub with an unprepossessing exterior turns out to be a little gem. This is your guide to some of the best traditional pubs in Lancashire*: where to find them; what kind of pubs they are; what beers are  available and what type of food is on offer. Also parking arrangements, unusual opening and closing times, family facilities and pub entertainments are covered.

There is every type of pub you could wish for here but they do have certain things in common: in general they remain true to their origins and have not been altered too much by the brewery. They often retain the multi-room plan form once typical of northern pubs and they demonstrate true hospitality by catering for all types and all ages of customers.

Any Lancashire pub which is notable for its impressive or unusual interior has been included in the guide.

How To Use The Guide

Location

The County is divided into four areas:

Manchester Area;

Liverpool and South Lancashire;

Ribble, Calder, Pendle Area;

West Lancashire and Furness.

* the original Lancashire, pre-1974, which has the River Mersey as a southern boundary and includes the Furness area of Cumbria.

Each town, suburb or village is listed alphabetically and the address and directions to the whereabouts of each pub are given. The main entries in each area are followed by a list and a brief description of other pubs worth visiting. All the locations of the main entry pubs can be found on the county map on pages 22–23. In larger towns and cities you will sometimes find a street map is useful to avoid getting lost. Some pubs which are really off the beaten track are given an Ordnance Survey reference. An indication of parking provision is given for each pub except those in the city centre areas of Manchester and Liverpool.

Real Ale

 These days real ale is available in about 75% of pubs and in Lancashire, with its rich brewing heritage, you will invariably find it to be a distinctive quality product, unlike some other areas of the country. There is nothing mysterious about real ale, or cask-conditioned beer as it is also known. It is simply beer which has not been pasteurised or filtered and when it is delivered to the pub it is not ready to drink so it requires some skill and care to keep it and then serve it in peak condition. With two exceptions all the pubs in the guide serve real ale.

Opening Times

Opening times tend to vary from pub to pub depending on local habits and in tourist areas and the countryside there is often a seasonal variation. Pubs are normally permitted to open between 11am and 11pm Monday to Saturday but most of them close for two or three hours in the afternoon. Standard Sunday hours are 12 noon to 3pm and 7pm to 10.30pm. If a pub opens at unusual times or is closed on any day of the week, this is mentioned. If there are no comments on opening times it means that you can expect to find the pub open at lunchtime from 12 noon at least but possibly earlier and from 6pm in the evenings but possibly earlier.

Beers and other drinks

For each pub, all the beers normally available are listed. Traditional cider and anything unusual such as foreign bottled beers or a good range of wines or whiskies are also mentioned.

This is primarily a pub guide rather than a beer guide and, although you would normally expect good pubs to have good licensees who know how to look after their beer, licensees do come and go and beer quality can change (for better or worse) overnight. The **CAMRA Good Beer Guide** is of course the guide to the best beer and if you are armed with both this book and the GBG you cannot go wrong!

Food

Food is a rapidly growing part of pub business and it is usually much better value for money than High Street restaurants. Some of it is run-of-the-mill with unimaginative menus, food often frozen and microwaved and ingredients from convenience, mass catering sources. But occasionally, where there are discerning customers, some pubs try a bit harder and produce good quality 'home cooked' style meals and every now and then you can come across a place which exhibits real flair and people are prepared to beat a path to their door.

Each pub entry here gives information on food availability at lunchtimes and evenings; whether full meals or snacks are available; some indication of the type of food and a rough idea of price levels.

Family facilities

The situation with regard to children in pubs is often unclear and there is some polarity of opinion on the matter. On the one hand there are claims that there should be no reason why children cannot be catered for in licensed premises just as they are in other European countries and on the other hand there is the feeling that the English pub is quite different from continental bars and cafes, is traditionally a place for adults and should remain so. The debate continues and in the meantime it is difficult to establish any ground rules.

In practice some pubs prefer no children under any circumstances; many consider that the best place for children is outside the pub in the beer garden (which is alright as long as the weather is fine); some tolerate children if they accompany parents for a meal; some reserve a special room or separate area for children; occasionally there is a relaxed and welcoming atmosphere for families.

The comments for each pub try to give some indication of what to expect in this regard but the only way to be sure is to pop in, in advance, and ask the licensee for guidance.

Pub Entertainment

Music in pubs is another bone of contention to many people. The comments give an indication of what you might find in the way of live entertainment (including sing songs and karaoke) and when it is on. Also the presence of juke boxes and fruit machines is mentioned and whether there are any rela-tively noise-free areas you can escape to if you wish.

Lancashire Breweries and their Beers

A Beer Drinker's Paradise

Forty years ago, there were over 40 breweries operating in Lancashire and of these only 10 remain but a further 10 small companies have appeared on the scene during the last few years. Between them they produce over 70 regular beers plus a further 15 or so occasional brews. Where else in the country can claim this diversity of choice over a comparable area? And what choice! – probably any kind of beer you could wish for is available here ranging from powerful winter ales as strong as wine to refreshing, quaffable milds and light bitters. The brewer's ingenuity has been stretched to the limits to produce such complex combinations of flavours, colours, aromas and lingering after tastes.

The following pages give some brief background on each brewery and the real ales they produce plus one or two distinctive non-real bottled beers. The percentage alcohol by volume (ABV) is given for each beer as an indication of its strength. Broadly speaking milds and light bitters are usually in the range 3% to 3.5% ABV; bitters, 3% to 4% ABV; best bitters 4.1% to 4.5% ABV and premium bitters, 4.6% to 5.5% ABV. Anything above this is classed as a strong ale. For those who are interested in detailed tasting notes on the beers, see the **Good Beer Guide** or the **Real Ale Drinker's Almanac**, both published by CAMRA.

'Not Lancashire Breweries'

First a mention of those breweries whose liveries are quite widespread in Lancashire but whose beers are in fact now brewed in foreign parts. Once famous beers such as **Higsons** of Liverpool and **Chesters** of Manchester are now brewed at the Whitbread plant in Sheffield. **Higsons** mild and bitter can still be obtained in the ex-Higson pubs of Merseyside but the beers are generally reckoned to be a pale shadow of their former character and the bitter is gradually being supplanted by the local **Cains** bitter. **Chesters** pubs these days often sell anything but **Chesters** beers. It is a brand which was re-introduced by Whitbread in the early 1980s. The bitter is becoming harder to find now, which is no great loss, but so also is the mild, which is appreciated by many mild drinkers.

Wilsons beers were brewed in Manchester until 1986, when production was transferred to Halifax. The brand is now part of the Courage empire and the future for the beers is uncertain. Both the mild and the bitter have their devotees in their local area but the number of outlets is slowly declining. **Matthew Brown** was once a proud independent Blackburn brewery who took over the Yorkshire based Theakston Brewery in 1984 and

were themselves taken over, on the third attempt in 1987, by Scottish and Newcastle Breweries. Mild and Bitter bearing the **Matthew Brown** name are now brewed in Nottingham but the beer seems set to be phased out and Theakstons' brands (sometimes brewed in their home town of Marsham and sometimes in Newcastle) are being marketed in their place.

Lancashire Breweries

Boddingtons Strangeways Brewery, Manchester

The brand image of the famous **Boddingtons Bitter** (ABV 3.8%) became such hot property that the company felt unable to develop it to its full potential with their limited North West base and, in 1989, sold their breweries to Whitbread (but kept hold of their pubs). So far, Whitbread have kept Boddingtons in Manchester, expanded production to the limits of existing capacity and, if anything, have improved the consistency of the beer.

You are liable to come across the bitter in all sorts of outlets these days, mainly in the North West but gradually finding its way further afield: in Boddington Pub Company pubs, freehouses, Whitbread pubs and wherever the tentacles of the Whitbread conglomerate can reach.

The strong brand image and the aggressive marketing virtually guarantees sales, regardless of the merits of the beer but how does it actually rate? In certain quarters some people feel very emotive about Boddingtons Bitter because the taste and characteristics of the beer changed a couple of decades ago, because the company became predatory (acquiring Oldham Brewery and then Higsons) and finally because they sold a part of Manchester's heritage to Whitbread.

It is all true but on the other hand, the beer is still regarded by many as a good distinctive brew and, in a recent CAMRA report, Michael Hardman, an ex-Mancunian and one of the founders of CAMRA, said that, although the romance of drinking Boddingtons had gone, in a blind tasting it would still rate highly.

Also brewed at Strangeways: **OB Bitter** (ABV 3.8%), a former Oldham Brewery beer with a strong following in the Oldham area, and **Boddingtons Mild** (ABV 3%) and **OB Mild** (ABV 3%), two very quaffable milds but unfortunately, in common with most milds and light bitters, suffering from a decline in demand.

Burtonwood Brewery, Burtonwood Village, Near Warrington

The founder of the brewery, James Forshaw, is said to have acquired pubs along the route between Warrington and his holiday retreat in Wales. A third of Burtonwood's 260 pubs are in Wales and they have recently bought pubs in Yorkshire and Humberside also. The brewery is still 48% owned by the descendants of James

Forshaw and is virtually takeover-proof. Over the last few years around £7 million has been spent on rebuilding the brewery and it is now a high tech, computerised operation. **Burtonwood Dark Mild** (ABV 3.1%) seems to be going strong and both the mild and the **Burtonwood Best Bitter** (ABV 3.7%) can also be found in some Courage John Smith pubs.

The company keep trying to launch a premium bitter. Two previous attempts have fizzled out but the latest product is **James Forshaw's Bitter** (ABV 4%), a distinctive brew which may be marketed as a guest beer to the large national brewers.

Robert Cain and Company, Stanhope Street Brewery, Liverpool

There was a tremendous fuss when Whitbread closed the Higsons brewery in Liverpool in 1990 and for a while the Merseyside beer scene looked very bleak with so-called Higsons beers being produced in Yorkshire and otherwise an over dependence on Tetley Walker of Warrington. However, the brewery was bought by an intrepid little company who renamed it after its founder back in 1848 and began to produce **Cains Traditional Bitter** (ABV 3.8%) and **Cains Formidable Ale** (ABV 5.1%).

In fairy tale fashion the future of the brewery has since been assured, firstly by an agreement with the Boddington Pub Company to take Cains beers in its Merseyside pubs, and secondly when the Danish company Faxe Jyske bought a controlling interest in the brewery in order to produce Scandia lager.

RAISE CAINS

· FIRST ESTABLISHED 1850 ·

Reviving Merseyside's Brewing Heritage

This ensures that the brewery operates at an efficient level and provides a degree of security which is otherwise lacking for brewing companies who do not own pubs. Then to compound the good fortune **Cains Bitter** won first prize in the ordinary bitter category of CAMRA's 1991 Champion Beer of Britain Competition.

Cains is a worthy successor to the Higsons that was. They are usually sold side by side which gives you a perfect opportunity to compare them and judge for yourself. You may also find a new brew to be introduced in 1992, **Cains Dark Mild**. Although the re-establishment of a Liverpool brewery seems the result of a chain of good fortune, in fact the process was helped along by the people of Liverpool, spearheaded by the local CAMRA branches, who refused to acquiesce to what was happening and campaigned until they got what they wanted.

Coach House Brewing Company, Warrington

After a 200 year tradition of brewing in Warrington, Greenall Whitley abandoned their breweries in 1991 and became a pub company like Boddingtons. The move was welcomed by many who felt that their lack-lustre beers could only improve if brewed by someone else (now brewed under contract by Tetley).

Another good thing to come out of all this is the Coach House operation, comprised of a few ex-Greenalls employees who pooled their redundancy resources, bought some of the Greenalls equipment and set up in a refurbished factory on the banks of the River Mersey. The two regular beers produced are **Coachmans Best Bitter** (ABV 3.7%) and **Innkeepers Special Reserve** (ABV

5%) and, after some inevitable teething problems both have been well received.

Sales are gradually building up, mainly through an arrangement with Greenalls to take the beers as guest beers in selected local outlets, but also through the free trade. Two further brews have recently been introduced, **Blunderbuss** (ABV 5.5%) for the winter and **Squires Gold** (ABV 4.2%) for the spring. In summer a low strength **Ostlers SPA** is expected and in autumn a **Taverners Autumn Ale** (ABV 5.5%).

Joseph Holt, Derby Brewery, Manchester

In a fast changing world it is very comforting to know of this small family firm who just carry on doing things in the traditional way they always have done, generally oblivious to current fads and fashions and only adapting to them when they have to, at a snail's pace. The brewery is run on very 'low tech' lines and they are happy to use bits of equipment discarded by other brewers.

The beer recipes have not changed for 30 years and the **Holt Mild** (ABV 3.2%) and **Holt Bitter** (ABV 4%) are both very distinctive beers, strong on hoppiness and bitterness. The mild is available in all but one of Holt's pubs. A very palatable bottled strong ale is also produced- **Sixex** (ABV 6%). Holts also have the distinction of providing the cheapest beer in the country, always about half the price you would be charged in London pubs, and yet manage to have the highest operating profit margin of any brewer in the country.

They are choosy about who they supply beer to and do not like it to be moved too far (all their 102 pubs are within a 15 mile radius of the brewery), but the free trade and guest beer trade is gradually expanding. Those astute enough to hold Holt shares over the last decade have been rewarded with steadily increasing profits and a tripling of the dividend.

All this does seems too good to be true so it is only fair to draw attention to the one thing which has harmed Holt's reputation – the modernisation of some of their pubs.

Over the years, while many of the larger breweries were wrecking their pubs, the Holt policy seemed to be 'if it ain't broke, don't fix it' and their many Edwardian pubs were only subject to the occasional redecoration and reupholstering, but more recently they seem to have a craze for gutting the interior of some pubs and spoiling appearances in others by knocking ugly, misproportioned and angular holes in the walls. However there are still quite a few unspoilt, traditional Holt pubs around and, despite their insularity, the company may eventually get the message that these pubs are an asset.

Hydes' Anvil Brewery, Manchester

Hydes also manage to produce a high operating profit percentage and are similar to Holts in other ways. The brewery is still owned and run by the fourth generation of the Hyde family and the fifth generation is beginning to become involved; their 60 pubs are also within a small radius of the brewery and they keep their prices relatively low.

Hydes like to emphasise that they are one of the few breweries who produce pure beer, using only malt, hops, yeast and water and, apart from a little gypsum to harden the water, spurn the use of additives or malt substitutes. Four beers are produced: **Bitter** (ABV 3.8%), **Mild** (ABV 3.5%, **Light** (ABV 3.7%) which is an alternative to the mild in many pubs and, in a rare few outlets, **Dark Mild** (ABV 3.5%) which is simply the **Light** with added caramel. A fifth beer, **Strong Ale** (ABV 8%), has not been produced for sometime and is under review but hopefully will appear for winter l992/3.

J. W. Lees, Greengate Brewery, Middleton

Lees' 175 pubs and clubs are mainly distributed in two clusters; around the brewery in the Middleton/Rochdale/Oldham area and in North Wales. This is another family owned company which was founded in 1828 by John Lees, a retired cotton manufacturer. Three distinctive beers are produced and sold at reasonable prices but quality tends to vary with Lees beers more than other local beers. The **GB Mild** (ABV 3%) and the **Bitter** (ABV 4%) are both generally available in all their pubs but the **Moonraker** (ABV 7.5%) can only be found in a few selected outlets. Moonrakers are yokels who attempt to rake in the moon (presumably after drinking too much of the stuff). Lees also produce an impressive, bottled **Harvest Ale** (ABV 12.5%), – but treat with caution.

Original Lion's Brews, Griffin Brewery, Burnley

Similar to the Coach House Brewery, this is another brave new venture set up with redundancy monies after the cessation of brewing at the Matthew Brown Brewery. The only beer so far is the **Lion's Bitter** (ABV 4%) which is being sold to the guest beer and freehouse trade. The company are proud to produce a good wholesome tasty beer at a low price, currently £1 per pint in many outlets.

Mitchell's, Lancaster

Mitchell's is yet another old-established family brewery, founded in Lancaster in 1880, which operates in a very traditional way with only 54 pubs plus many free trade outlets. They moved and took over the redundant Yates and Jackson brewery in Lancaster in 1985. Known as the 'Old Brewery', it has the date 1669 over the entrance and is a splendid example of traditional methods and machinery – not the sort of place where you will find stainless steel vessels and computerised controls. All the beers are brewed using natural spring well water.

The beers are well regarded too: **Dark Mild** (ABV 3.4%), **Best Bitter** (ABV 3.6%), **ESB (Extra Special Bitter)** (ABV 5%) and the seasonal winter beer, **Single Malt Winter Warmer** (ABV 7.5%), which is reminiscent of malt whisky in aroma and flavour. Two recent additions are **Old Priory Porter** (ABV3.4%) and **Fortress** (ABV 4.2%).

Moorhouse's Brewery, Burnley

In the last six years Moorhouse have more than doubled capacity to cope with the demand from their five tied houses (four in Burnley and one in Bury) and extensive pub and club free trade outlets over half of the county.

The brewery has actually been in existence since 1870, but until 1979 the business was in concentrated hop bitters which is used by the soft drinks trade to make shandy. The new beer brewing venture soon began to take off in 1983 when the **Premier bitter** (ABV 3.6%) won a Silver Medal at the International Brewing and Bottling Exhibition. Then, in 1989, the **Pendle Witches Brew** (ABV 5%) won a CAMRA Champion Beer of Britain award. Pendle Witch has almost a cult following. More recently the company has introduced a beautifully dry dark mild, **Black Cat Mild** (ABV 3.4%) and their seasonal winter brew is **Owd Ale** (ABV 6.4%).

Oak Brewing Company, Phoenix Brewery, Heywood (Nr. Rochdale)

The Oak Brewery started life in a factory unit in Ellesmere Port, Cheshire in 1982 and since then it has steadily developed its free trade and guest beer business throughout the north of England on the strength of its excellent brews. The Phoenix Brewery dates from 1898 but it had not been used as a brewery since 1940 until Oak took over and began production in 1991. The new premises will provide the much needed extra capacity. Oak produces no less than eight beers; **Hopwood Bitter** (ABV 3.4%, a new brew created at the new brewery), **Best Bitter** (ABV 3.8%), **Old Oak Ale** (ABV 4.4%), **Extra Double Stout** (ABV 4.5%, an occasional brew), **Double Dagger** (ABV 5%), **Porter** (ABV 5%) and **Wobbly Bob** (ABV 6%, named after the three legged brewery cat). The brewery also brews **Tyke Bitter** (ABV 4.2%) under contract for the West Riding Brewery, Yorkshire.

Frederic Robinson, Unicorn Brewery, Stockport

Stockport is of course just outside the old
Lancashire border, but Robinsons can
be counted as an honorary Lancashire brewery when so much of their
trade is in that area. This is a fine
traditional 1920s brewery operating
from virtually the same spot where
William Robinson began business
at the Unicorn Inn over 150 years
ago. Frederic Robinson established
the brewery sometime later.

The fifth generation are running the
brewery today in fiercely independent style,
and there seems to be little danger of take-over by a larger brewer.
The brewery still contains some of its original equipment but there
has also been much investment in modern plant in recent years.
The Robinsons have a rather paternalistic approach to their small
empire of 378 pubs (mainly in South Manchester and Cheshire)
and go their own idiosyncratic way, somewhat like Joseph Holt.

Their **Dark Best Mild** (ABV 3.3%) for example continues to be
supplied to only 2 pubs because there is still a demand for it.
Looking after your customers to this extent would be anathema to
the accountants who control the larger brewers. The **Best Mild**
(ABV 3.3%) can be found in most of their pubs and is unusual in

that it is light coloured and, to the
uninitiated, could be mistaken for
bitter. The **Bitter** (ABV 3.5%) is a
refreshing, low-gravity, session beer
but is only available in about 20
outlets. The **Best Bitter** (ABV 4.2%)
is usually good value for money for
a beer of this strength. The most
distinctive beer though is the **Old
Tom** (ABV 8.5%), brewed since
1899, a truly classic strong ale,
vinous and complex.

In 1982, Robinsons acquired the **Hartleys** Brewery of Ulverston and lost a few friends there in 1991 when they decided to close it down. The Hartleys production was transferred to Stockport but the range of beers been pared down. Robinsons have also attracted much adverse comment on the treatment of their pubs but it does not seem to have got through to them yet.

Tetley Walker, Warrington

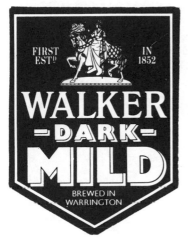

In 1960, Joshua Tetley of Leeds merged with Walker Cain of Warrington and in 1961 the group became part of the Allied Breweries conglomerate. The Warrington Brewery (Tetley Walker) serves the western side of the Pennines and the Leeds Brewery, (Joshua Tetley) supplies Yorkshire. Since 1990, when Greenall Whitley ceased brewing, the Warrington brewery has also produced Greenalls beers for the Greenalls pub group and this has brought the brewery up to full capacity production and ensured its survival.

Altogether 10 beers are now produced at Warrington for the Lancashire market. **Tetley Dark Mild** (ABV 2.9%, introduced in 1990), **Tetley Mild** (ABV 3.15%), **Greenalls Mild** (ABV 3.1%), **Walker Mild** (ABV 2.9%, considered by many to be the best of the milds from Warrington), **Tetley Bitter** (ABV 3.6%). **Walker Bitter** (ABV 3.3%, more like a light mild than a bitter), **Walker Best Bitter** (ABV 3.6%), **Greenalls Bitter** (ABV 3.8%, much improved since it has been brewed by Tetleys), **Walker Winter Warmer** (ABV 5.8%, a seasonal beer which improves with age) and finally **Thomas Greenall's Original Bitter** (ABV 4.4%, proudly introduced by Greenalls not long before they finished brewing, tends to be variable). 173 of Tetley Walker pubs serve real ale including all 91 Peter Walker pubs.

You can't beat 'em.

Daniel Thwaites, Star Brewery, Blackburn

Thwaites are the largest of the independent brewers in the North West with around 400 pubs in Lancashire, almost all selling real ale. The brewery tower is a major landmark in Blackburn and, although the brewery has been extensively modernised in recent years, the company see themselves as upholders of brewing tradition and they still use horse drawn drays to deliver in the locality of the brewery.

The brewery was established in 1807 and is still controlled by the descendants of Daniel Thwaites. The beers have won many prizes at CAMRA beer festivals. They are: **Mild** (ABV 3%), **Best Mild** (ABV 3.2%, produced mainly for the Preston area), **Bitter** (ABV 3.4%, described as the archetypal North West bitter in the Real Ale Drinkers Almanac), a brand new brew, **Craftsman Ale** (ABV 4.2%) and **Daniels Hammer** (ABV 5%, a strong winter ale).

West Coast Brewery, Manchester

West Coast beers have made a big impact in the Manchester area since 1989 when the brewery was set up It is a very compact little brewery housed in the cellars of the Kings Arms Hotel.

All five regular beers are very distinctive and have been consistently so during the three years of operation. The brewery was founded by Irishman Brendan Dobbin who has worked as a brewery consultant all over the world and he claims, probably truthfully, that he can take any beer from anywhere in the world and replicate it in his cellar brewery.

The only place you can guarantee being able to sample all five beers is in the Kings Arms and, as it is difficult to find, even with an A to Z, a map is provided. (see the section on Manchester Freehouses – page 95)

You should begin with the full flavoured, **Dobbin's Dark Mild** (ABV 3%); progress onto the **Dobbin's Best Bitter** (ABC 4%, the most popular of the lot); graduate onto the **Dobbin's Guiltless Stout** (ABV 4%) and compare it to another famous Irish Stout in terms of taste and wholesomeness.

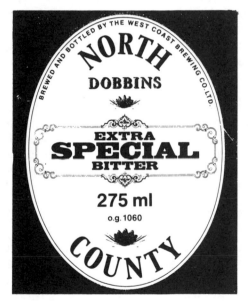

You will then be ready for the **Big Heavy Jimmy** (ABV 4.5%) and the **Dobbin's Yakima Grande Pale Ale** (ABV 6%), which is modelled on **Sierra Nevada Pale Ale**, a world class California beer originally modelled on the English brewing style!

Finally there is the powerful **Dobbin's Extra Special Bitter** (ABV 7%). However in winter you need not stop there because the seasonal brew is **Dobbin's Old Soporific** (ABV 10%) and probably the strongest draught beer mentioned on these pages – treat with caution. Away from the Kings Arms **Old Soporific** is available in bottled form in many freehouses.

Lancashire Brew Pubs

Nearly all the famous breweries started as brew pubs, brewing for a single outlet. If they are successful they inevitably grow, usually by expanding their trade locally and gradually building up until they became more of a brewery than a pub. Are any of these brew pubs destined to become the Holts and the Robinsons of the next century?

Black Horse and Rainbow, Berry Street, Liverpool

The brewery started in 1990. **Black Horse** (ABV 4.5%) is the regular beer and there are two or three seasonal brews during the year. The beer is not classed as real ale because it is kept in tanks under a blanket of carbon dioxide.

Flea and Firkin, 137 Grosvenor Street, Manchester

This brew pub is part of a national chain of brew pubs which began with the Goose and Firkin in London in 1979. They are all large, back-to-basics, spit and sawdust places with bare floorboards and a viewing area where you can watch the brewing process. The concept has been very successful with the result that it has become the property of leisure groups and has been bought and sold a few times.

The Flea and Firkin is housed in an old cinema, a listed building. It is very popular with students and is a good example of how to create instant atmosphere. The Flea and Firkin's brewer is dedicated to his craft and, although some beers have, in the past, not been kept in an entirely traditional way, his aim is to achieve 100% cask conditioned output as soon as possible.

There are four regular beers: **Scratch Bitter** (ABV 3.7%), **Grosvenor Bitter** (ABV 4.3%, named after the old cinema), **Dogholter** (ABV 5.9%) and a **Ginger Beer** (ABV 6.4%, brewed to a traditional recipe). In addition there is always a strong ale which is varied now and then. The current version is **Leap Year Ale** (ABV 8% to 8.8%) and usually a **stout** which varies in strength depending on the season. A strong **Pale Ale** will be produced for the summer months. The motto of the Firkin chain is, appropriately, *Usque Ad Mortem Bibendum.*

Lass O'Gowrie, Charles Street, Manchester

This pub is also popular with students. It is a Whitbread tied pub which uses malt extract instead of a proper barley mash in the brewing process. The two regular beers are **Log 35** (ABV 3.5%) and **Log 42** (ABV 4.2%) and there are two further occasional beers; **Centurion** (ABV 5.2%, brewed twice per year) and **Graduation** (ABV 5.6%, obviously brewed once per year).

Thomas McGuiness Brewery Company, Cask and Feather, Oldham Road, Rochdale

This is a brand new brewing operation, started in 1992 and supplying three pubs in Rochdale plus the free trade in the Manchester area. The first beer proudly bears the owner's name, **Thomas McGuiness Best Bitter** (ABV 3.8%). There are plans for two further bitters, a stout and a porter and the intention is to produce wholesome, traditionally brewed beers at reasonable prices.

Masons Arms, Strawberry Bank, Cartmel Fell

The Masons Arms is famous as a pub and is listed in the West Lancashire and Furness section of this guide but it is also a brewery and must be mentioned here also. The home brewed beers regularly available are **Amazon Bitter** (ABV 3.8%), **Great Northern Bitter** (ABV 4.1%), **Big Six** (ABV 6%) and a Belgian-style **Damson Kriek Beer** (ABV 9%). Some of the beers are named after titles by Arthur Ransome, the local children's author.

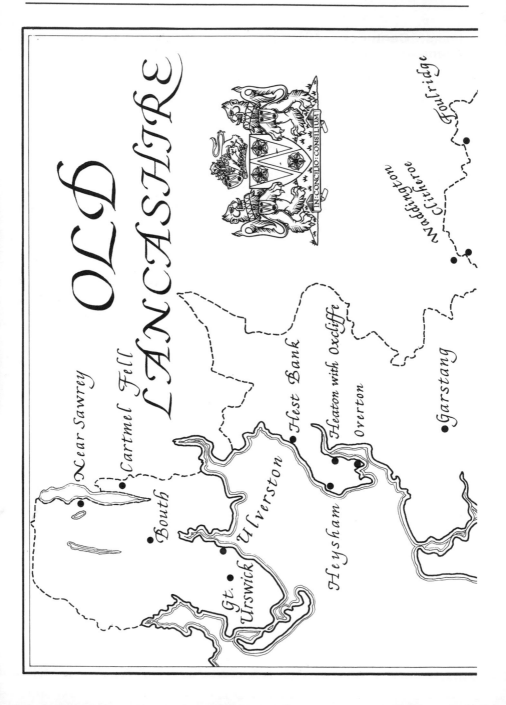

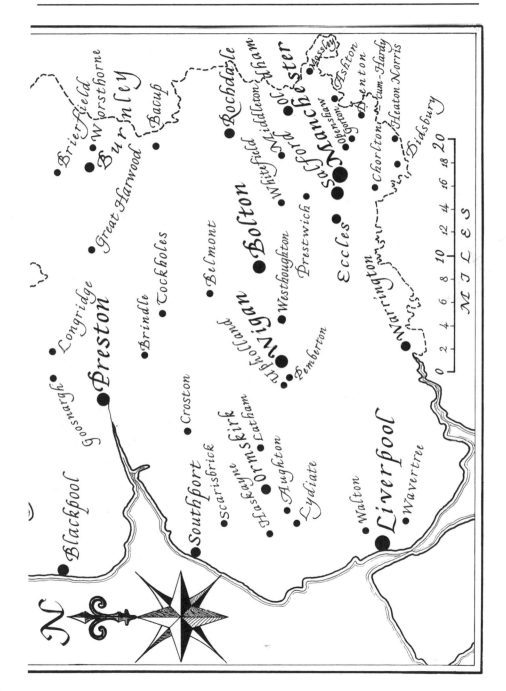

The Circus Tavern, Manchester City Centre

Manchester

ASHTON-UNDER-LYNE

Oddfellows Arms

Kings Road, Hurst

Off B6194, Lees Road, off A670, northeast of town centre.

Street parking available

Robinson's Best Mild, Best Bitter

If only every street corner pub was like the **Oddfellows,** then there would be no need for this guide. What makes the pub special is

the intimate layout of spaces and small rooms with many original fittings and the unstinting approach to hospitality – nothing is too good for the customers. The pub dates from before 1830 and over the years it has gradually expanded to occupy three cottages. Since 1914 it has been very personally run by three generations of the same family. You enter past a small hatch and screen which would have been an outdoor department. There is a lobby area with a few nooks and crannies in front of the bar and radiating off, a tap room, snug (known as the 'vestry'), lounge and, off the lounge, 'Toms Room', created out of private quarters and named after the last family member to run the pub. The bar has a fine stained glass front and there is much original bench seating – simple settle type and a comfortable padded version in the lounge.

All the rooms are furnished in a style and quality good enough for anyone's best sitting room. The licensee's family photographs do not look out of place. There are three open fires, a television in the tap room, low volume piped music (sometimes the local radio station) and the whole effect creates a very comfortable and relaxing atmosphere. At lunchtimes sandwiches and pies are available and there is always a daily special costing about £1. In summer there are occasional barbecues in the beer garden.

Being in the heart of a large residential area, the pub's role is obviously to serve the local community but visitors are made welcome. Make sure you visit the toilets while you are here because they have just won the 1991 'Initial' award for the best pub toilets in the North of England!

BOLTON

Howcroft

Clarence Court

First right off Vernon Street, off St Georges Road, north of town centre.

Street parking

Walker Mild, Best Bitter

Evening opening 7pm in winter

The **Howcroft** is a former beerhouse dating from the late 18th century and formed out of a pair of terraced houses. It is still a good old fashioned back street local even though the back street has disappeared to be replaced by a modern court of houses and apartments. The pub won a CAMRA award in 1986 in recognition of the sensitive refurbishment work undertaken by the brewery.

They simply made the most of what was there, echoing the simple style of the place and not trying to improve on it. There is a central bar and standing up area and a vault, a snug and large lounge all separated by attractive wooden panelled and half glazed partitions with a bit of coloured glass embellishment. It is decorated in creams, ambers and dark brown to reflect the wholesome colours of Walkers beers and furnished with simple, traditional pub furniture.

The **Howcroft** serves the local community well and much activity is focused on the bowling green. The green was actually in existence as early as 1842 and the pub was built alongside it. During redevelopment of the area in the early 1980s it was realigned to its present position at the rear of the pub. In summer there are tables and chairs around the green. Snacks and home made meals are available lunchtimes and early evenings. Meals cost around £2. Smaller portions are available for children.

BOLTON

Sweet Green Tavern

127 Crook Street

Just off Trinity Street, west of BR Station.

There is some limited parking space on Crook Street

Tetley Mild, Bitter; Hydes' Bitter

Situated at a busy crossroads near the town centre, the **Sweet Green Tavern** is a survivor from a different age. It has evolved from one of those typical corner pubs formed out of a couple of terraced properties many years ago. All the surrounding houses have been demolished to form new roads and the pub, now surrounded by traffic, is a welcome haven from the city bustle. It has obviously seen many alterations and refurbishments over the

years but the result is a pleasing mixture of old and new which is
familiar and comfortable.

There are no less than six separate areas radiating out from a
central bar so, for those who want to, it is nearly always possible to
find a quiet corner. There are also seats and tables outside,
screened from the traffic, for the fine weather. Snacks and pub
meals are available at lunchtimes. The local CAMRA beer guide
describes the place as *'a superb pub with a truly local feel to it'*.
The name must have some association with the time, 170 years
ago, when this part of Bolton was known for its orchards and
gardens. Football fans take note that there is a notice in the
window stating SORRY NO 'AWAY SUPPORTERS' THANK YOU.

BOLTON

Ye Olde Man and Scythe

6 Churchgate

Town Centre, off Bradshawgate, near Deansgate

Parking nearby is difficult

Boddingtons Bitter; Trophy Bitter; Flowers IPA (beers liable to change). Also a range of traditional ciders are available.

With its black and white timber framing and low eaves the **Man and Scythe** looks its part as an ancient and venerable public house. There has been an inn on the site since 1251 and some of the fabric may date back to then, but this building dates from 1636. During the English civil war, Bolton was captured by the Royalists under the leadership of James Stanley, the 7th Earl of Derby and the local people were made to suffer. Their turn came when in

1651 the Earl was captured at the battle of Worcester and brought back to Bolton to be executed. He spent his last hours at the **Man and Scythe** and was beheaded at the market cross in Churchgate on 15 October 1651. At one time the pub was part of the Pilkington family estate and the name of the pub is borrowed from the Pilkington family crest.

Inside the pub the low ceilings, narrow spaces and sloping floors still give an impression of antiquity but it has also been brought into the 20th century with reproduction fireplaces (unused), plush carpeting and upholstery and a juke box. It is a rakish sort of pub, frequented by Bolton characters. Nobody takes any notice of the 'no standing at the bar' sign; there are posters advertising 'Ann Summers Nights' for ladies and the juke box music penetrates all three rooms: public bar, front parlour and lounge. A wide range of sandwiches and snacks are available at around £1 to £1.50 and full meals (including breakfast and steak and cowheel pie) cost £2 to £2.70.

CHORLTON-CUM-HARDY

Beech

72 Beech Road, Chorlton Green

Beech Road is off the A5145, next to Chorlton bus terminus

Chesters Bitter; Taylor Landlord

The **Beech** is where the Chorlton cognoscenti gather. The great thing about this pub is that it does not change and this is quite an achievement in Chorlton where a couple of pubs have recently undergone their second re-Victorianisation. A painting of the pub in 1927, displayed inside, shows it with a Threlfalls Brewery hoarding, some stained glass panels in the windows and an ornate lamp. All these have disappeared but otherwise the building is pretty much the same. It was built originally as a Methodist school in the 1800s and was later converted to residential use and then eventually into a pub.

There is a vault at the back with separate entrance, a central bar and two front rooms. It is a simple, unpretentious place, and it attracts a cross section of people from a wide area because it is such a little oasis in a traditional pub desert. There is a television in the vault and juke box and fruit machine near the bar but if it gets noisy the third room remains relatively tranquil. Chorlton Green and Beech Road still have something of a village atmosphere and in summer it is pleasant to sit at tables in front of the pub. The Beech is within a Conservation Area which should give it a measure of protection from unsympathetic treatment by the brewery.

DENTON

Red Lion Hotel

1 Stockport Road, Crown Point

Main A57/A6017 junction in the centre of Denton

Market car park nearby.

Hydes' Light, Bitter

An inn has stood here since 1790, but this building dates from 1926. It was traditionally a hatters pub where commercial travellers met the hat manufacturers of Denton and the original layout of central bar with serving hatches to different parts of the pub helped to ensure privacy for those commercial transactions. The bar has been moved to the side of the pub and the interior has been opened out to some extent but it is still attractive and there are five distinct rooms and separated areas.

Comfortable traditional furnishings are combined with 1920s style leaded glass and wooden fittings of the period including an open staircase and two fireplaces with open fires. There is also an unusual domed skylight in the central area with a glass chandelier. There is a television in the main lounge and unobtrusive piped music. The customers are a wide cross section of local shoppers and business people during the day and a good mixture of locals in the evening. The pub is usually busier on market days — Wednesdays, Fridays and Saturdays and on those days the food servery offers good value typical pub grub.

DIDSBURY
Royal Oak

729 Wilmslow Road

Centre of village, opposite police station

It is difficult to park close by

Marston's Burton Bitter, Pedigree; Banks's Mild

The **Royal Oak** is a renowned pub of character, firmly rooted in the local community and very personally run by a long standing licensee. The first thing to greet you as you enter is an enormous pile of cheeses on a serving table in front of the bar for this pub is famous for its ploughmans lunches (it features in the CAMRA Good Pub Food Guide) and its exceptional collection of English and Continental cheeses including goats, ewes and smoked varieties. For a little over £2 you receive an enormous portion of cheese with home-baked bread plus a 'doggie bag' to take the surplus home with you. In winter, hot soup is available also.

However, even if you visit in the evenings, when food is not available, it is still a great pub. There are three rooms comfortably furnished with a mixed collection of solid old furniture and the walls are covered with old theatrical posters and Bass wall plaques dating from its days as a Bass pub. There is also an extensive collection of ceramic spirit vats, some nice old brewery mirrors and shelves full of Toby jugs and tankards. The character has been carefully preserved and every aspect in the running of the pub is handled with some verve and pride. At lunchtimes lady shoppers pop in for a whisky and soda; in the evenings there is a waitress service to some rooms and it is so popular that people often spill out onto the pavement. There is certainly no room, nor any need, for a juke box or fruit machine.

Interior of the Royal Oak

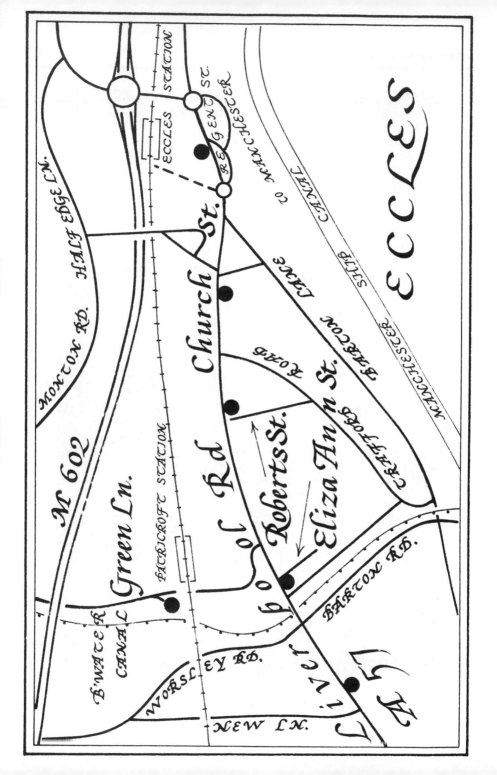

ECCLES

Crown and Volunteer

171 Church Street

A57, just west of Eccles town centre

Small car park adjacent

Holt Mild, Bitter

Eccles is famous for its pubs and is much visited by beer and pub aficionados. Unlike many other areas, the Eccles pub scene has always thrived. No pubs have been lost since a bomb destroyed the Golden Lion in 1941 and that was rebuilt in the sixties. A few extra pubs have appeared in recent years. About 30 different beers are available in the 51 real ale pubs. So there was quite a fuss when, in 1991, a proposed new road scheme threatened to demolish the **Crown and Volunteer** and the **Royal Oak** around the corner. A vigorous campaign was mounted,led by CAMRA,and the council planning committee took note of the concern and re-routed the road.

The **Crown and Volunteer** is a little gem. An unspoilt, popular pub built in 1939 in that neat and functional but attractive 1930s style and most of the original features are intact. There is much leaded glass in 1930s fashion, an original fireplace and an original feature ceiling lighting panel and whatever work has been done over the years has been generally sympathetic to the style of the pub. It is a real community pub with a busy social scene. Darts is played on both types of boards among four different teams on three nights of the week. It is only a two room pub and there is a darts board in each room. There is also a long established sea angling club. There is no juke box and no food.

ECCLES

Grapes Hotel

431 Liverpool Road, Peel Green

Just east of Junction 2, M63

Car park on former bowling green at side of pub

Holt Mild, Bitter

The Joseph Holt brewery embarked on an ambitious rebuilding programme in the early years of the century, mainly in Prestwich,

Salford and Eccles and all their pubs of this period are large distinctive red brick buildings with much decorative detail. In most cases the interiors have since been altered but the three pubs in Eccles: **Grapes, Lamb q.v.** and **Royal Oak** have all been spared from excessive 'improvements'. The **Grapes** is the most spacious and the most extravagant in its use of mahogany, cut and etched glass and dark green Art Nouveau tiling and the whole building is remarkably well preserved.

The vault is still a true public bar with the main bar counter. The lobby area with an open staircase and the billiard room with its fine 'Jacobethan' fireplace are the most impressive areas of the pub but the bar parlour and the smoke room (plus its extension into former private quarters) also have character allied with comfort. Successive redecorations have been carried out without spoiling the overall effect. Upstairs there is a well used clubroom which has not changed for decades. The pub serves the extensive residential areas around but it also attracts visitors from afar because of its architectural character. There is no juke box. Lunchtime food consists of sandwiches, burgers and salads and the most expensive item is £1.50.

ECCLES

Lamb Hotel

33 Regent Street

A57, Salford side of town centre

Car park at rear and side

Holt Mild, Bitter

The **Lamb** is quite a famous pub. It is a TV star, having featured in many television scenes including 'Coronation Street' and 'Bulman' but apart from that it is widely and affectionately known simply for being a good pub. It always appears busy soon after opening time; it attracts a broad range of people from near and far; there are four

separate rooms each with a different character and the atmosphere is enhanced by a feast of Edwardian mahogany, tiling and
decorative glass. There is a relatively spartan vault with a
television, a cosy bar parlour, a large lounge opening off a lobby
area and a billiards room with one of the last remaining full size
pub snooker tables in Manchester. Filled rolls are available
lunchtimes and early evening.

It is hard to believe that once, many years ago, the magnificent
mahogany bar and the Edwardian wall tiling were covered with a
few layers of paint. Luckily no lasting damage was done. It was
cleaned up by an enlightened tenant and today, to many people,
the **Lamb** represents the epitome of the English pub because of its
conviviality, the cheap, well kept Holt beers and its proximity to a
host of other good pubs in Eccles – what more could you want?

ECCLES

Queens Arms

Canal Bank, Green Lane

Beside Patricroft Railway Station, approach up a ramp
alongside Green Lane

Car park at top of ramp

Boddingtons Mild, Bitter

The **Queens Arms** became a listed building, at the instigation of
CAMRA, because of its historical associations. It is thought to have
been built in 1828 to coincide with the building of the Liverpool-
Manchester Railway. It is not on the street; it is adjacent to the
permanent way and, as the railway line was the first engine-hauled
passenger railway in the world, the **Queens** must be the world's
first railway pub. In those days Mancunians would take the train to
Eccles for a day out and refresh themselves at the pub with Eccles

Cakes and ale. In 1836 the pub benefited from the building of the Nasmyth Foundry (which housed the world's first steam hammer) situated immediately to the north.

The original name was the **Patricroft Tavern** but this was changed to honour the 1857 visit of Queen Victoria when she alighted at Patricroft Station and proceeded along the Bridgewater Canal by horse drawn barge to Worsley Hall (one of the horses fell into the canal).

The pub has adapted to modern times but has kept its original four room layout with a bar serving a vault and the other three rooms located away from the bar off a corridor. It is comfortable and homely with open fires in winter (one room has a distinctive Art Nouveau chimney piece) and in summer you can sit outside and watch the trains go by in a little south-facing suntrap. In addition to the regular locals, it is the sort of pub which attracts devotees from far and wide who appreciate its special atmosphere. Pies and sandwiches are available at lunchtimes.

ECCLES

Stanley Arms

295 Liverpool Road, Patricroft

A57, near Bridgewater Canal

Street parking nearby

Holt Mild, Bitter

The **Stanley** was built in the 1850s and it has seen very little change since then apart from necessary decoration and refurbishment. The vault is the heart of the pub. The original layout is retained with the bar counter taking up a corner of the room. The remainder of the pub is served from a hatch. The main door, opening straight off the street is invitingly wide open in summer. It is a community pub but strangers are not unwelcome.

If you enter through the side door you find yourself in a green tiled corridor decorated with local archive photographs. A small comfortable snug with a piano and a juke box is opposite the bar hatch, and at the end of the corridor a former private room with an old fashioned kitchen range has become the pool room. 'Stanley' was the family name of the Earls of Derby and the Holts connection comes from the siting of the brewery on the Earl's Cheetham estate. At weekends the whole pub can become quite crowded including the corridor. For food, filled rolls are usually available at all times.

ECCLES
White Lion

133 Liverpool Road, Patricroft

A57, corner of Roberts Street

Car park at rear

Holt Mild, Bitter

Michael Jackson of TV 'Beer Hunter' fame in his book 'The English Pub' mentions the **White Lion** as an example of Manchester pubs which have often escaped the worst excesses of 'interior design'. The pub dates back to 1864 and, although there has been some recent remodelling you can hardly tell and it appears to be virtually untouched. The vault was enlarged which is unusual these days to say the least.

There are some nice original features including much etched glass and some grained woodwork. In addition to the vault there is a central corridor for standing up drinking, a back room for darts and the lounge/music room which comes alive at weekends when a pianist plays all the old favourites and all assembled sing along with him. It is the sort of pub where you might be in danger of sitting in somebody's favourite seat where they always sit every Friday night but don't worry, they are friendly enough. The pub does not serve food.

GORTON

Hare and Hounds

187 Abbey Hey Lane

Abbey Hey Lane winds between Ashton Old Road (A655) and Hyde Road (A57).The pub is nearest to Ashton Old Road

Boddingtons Bitter; Chesters Mild

If you want to visit a genuine, unspoilt back street local, try the **Hare and Hounds**. The pub would still be familiar to the veterans of the 1947 mens picnic whose photograph hangs in the vault. It is a simple, no-frills pub, but everything in it has been well cared for and cherished.

You enter into a lobby with simple but attractive wall and floor tiles and a bar, and the small smoke room and back snug, which has been enlarged into a lounge, are off the lobby. The furniture is solid old Britannia tables and stools and wooden benches in the vault. The walls and ceilings are decorated in shades of brown and tan — beer shades — always the best traditional colours for a pub. Entertainment is provided by an old fashioned 'Fiesta' juke box in the snug and in the vault a television, together with darts and cribbage. The three fireplaces contain gas fires (no trendy coal fires here!). In the summer the tables and play equipment on the cleared grassy area by the side of the pub is popular with families. The **Hare and Hounds** plays a vital role in the local community. There are three football teams, ladies and mens darts teams and a social club which organises trips to European beer festivals. In the vault is a very well stocked trophy cabinet.

HEATON NORRIS
Nursery Inn

Green Lane

Off Heaton Moor Road, between A6 and A5145. The lane turns to the right at the end and becomes a cul-de-sac.

The pub has its own car park

Hydes' Mild, Bitter

The **Nursery** is a rather special pub. It was built in 1939, replacing a mid 19th century pub, and is therefore the youngest pub in this guide. It is a very suburban pub and quite genteel, situated in the heart of leafy South Manchester suburbia. The approach is along a narrow, cobbled cul-de-sac, reinforcing the impression of exclusivity. The pub is virtually as it was built incorporating 20th century standards of comfort and convenience but with old fashioned solid and durable standards of construction and a clean, spacious and unembellished design. There is generous use of light oak including full height panelling in the lounge and the leaded glass windows are decorated with an occasional coloured glass panel depicting a horticultural nursery motif — a spade, a watering can or a flower. In addition to the large lounge there is a bar lobby area, a smoke room/dining room, a vault with a separate entrance and a function room/dining room upstairs.

The pub has a few sporting connections. There is an immaculate bowling green at the rear and a thriving bowling club with a case full of trophies and a commemorative plaque of presidents since 1917. The pub football team also has a collection of trophies and the **Nursery** has the distinction of having been the first headquarters of Stockport County AFC when the club's ground was nearby.

Food is important here. Monday to Friday a range of starters, snacks and typical pub meals are available with waitress service. Also there is a choice of daily specials often featuring more exotic or foreign dishes. The menu is more limited at weekends. Meal prices are in the £3 to £3.50 range. It is good value for money and in fact the pub features in the CAMRA Good Pub Food Guide. Families with children can sit by the bowling green in fine weather otherwise on weekdays children are allowed in the upstairs dining room for a meal.

MANCHESTER CITY CENTRE
Briton's Protection

50 Great Bridgewater Street

Corner of Mosley Street, next to G–MEX

Jennings Bitter; Tetley Bitter; Robinson's Best Bitter; Ind Coope Burton Ale, plus an occasional guest beer

Closed Sunday lunchtime

The **Briton's Protection** sets out to be a superior, up-market establishment on a par with **Mr Thomas's** in Manchester City Centre but more hospitable. The drinks are not cheap but you can pay far more in some city centre establishments for much less. The building dates from 1811 and it has been a pub since 1820. The interior underwent an extensive refit during the 1920's and, despite a 1980's refurbishment by the brewery, the pub has retained its multi room layout and traditional ambience.The special character is much enhanced by the fastideous care heaped upon the place by the present licensees.

A long central bar in what was originally the vault at the front of the pub dispenses a good range of beers and also a wide selection of wines, champagnes and whiskeys. Behind the bar are two cosy parlours cum-dining rooms both served from hatches. All the original wall tiling, leaded glass, polished wooden doors, screens and fireplaces with open fires, look as good as the day they were installed and the few modern additions and changes have been made to blend in well. There are no juke boxes or gaming machines. For the summer months, there is a makeshift beer garden at the rear.

The lunchtime food offers some unusual starters (soup of the moment, breaded camembert, smoked salmon Breton) at £1.75 and a selection of main dishes (including steak and kidney pie, goujons of plaice, ravioli and bacon) at £2-£3 plus sandwiches,

cherry scones and coffee. The clientele comes from all walks of life, professional and business people at lunchtime, Halle Orchestra crowds and some of the Hacienda set (just around the corner) in the evenings and various groups use the upstairs function room including the Manchester Astrology Society, Heritage Transport Group and Old Time Music Hall devotees.

MANCHESTER CITY CENTRE

Circus Tavern

86 Portland Street

Between Princess Street and Piccadilly

Tetley Bitter

Opening hours may contract on certain days and certain times of year when business is quiet.

Blessings on the **Circus Tavern**; may it never change. The building is part of a row of Georgian properties which at one time contained five pubs and only the **Circus** and the **Grey Horse** remain. It is a simple, unsophisticated pub which remains close to its beer house origins and the woodgrained matchboard interior partitions look unchanged for 100 years. The **Circus** is the smallest pub in the city with two tiny rooms and a minute bar squeezed into a space under the stairs. Half a dozen people make it appear busy and with 20 people it is positively crowded but if you appreciate this kind of pub you do not mind the crush.

The narrow corridor is a popular drinking area for the landlord and his cronies and the two rooms attract a varied clientele of both sexes and all ages. At lunchtime people bring in their own food and wash it down with Tetley bitter. The bar counter is not large enough to accommodate an extra handpump for mild and there is only sufficient space behind the bar for a few bottles of spirits and soft drinks. No lagers here and no wines either; no pool table, no juke box and no fruit machine – just the hum of conversation.

MANCHESTER CITY CENTRE
Hare and Hounds

46 Shude Hill

Near junction with High Street

Tetley Bitter

One of the few city centre pubs which is open all permitted hours including weekends. The **Hare and Hounds** is also one of the rare unaltered city centre pubs. It was a busy market pub until Smithfield Market moved out to Openshaw in the 1960s. The pub has broad appeal despite having only one real ale because people are attracted by its unspoilt 1920s interior and its tranquil atmosphere.

The brewery designers have recently been let loose on the place and, although they have installed the ubiquitous job lot of framed prints and archive photographs on the walls, they have respected and even complemented the original interior. The entrance corridor widens out into a spacious lobby area formed by the brown tiled walls and dark oak panelled bar with leaded glass screens. This part of the pub fills up first and acts as a sort of public bar. The rest of the pub comprises a relatively plain front room with a darts board and a back lounge, carpeted and with an open fire in winter. The lounge also contains an unusual glazed light well in the ceiling.

The pub functions like a local in the heart of town where you can play darts and cribbage or stand at the bar and, although there is piped music and the lounge has a television, the volume is turned down and conversation is easy. At lunchtime simple, reasonably priced snacks of toasties and granary bread with cheese or pate are available. Upstairs a large function room is available for hire and is used by various local groups and societies.

MANCHESTER CITY CENTRE

Mr Thomas's Chop House

52 Cross Street

Corner of St Ann's Passage

Boddingtons Bitter; Castle Eden Ale; extensive wine list also available

Closed Sunday.

This is an impressive building both inside and out though it tends to be dwarfed by its taller modern neighbours. It is a listed building, built in 1901 on the site of a famous Victorian Chop House dating from 1867. The exterior is in ornate Flemish style glazed brick and terracotta. The ground floor interior is a long gallery broken into three separate areas by arched dividing walls and the arch feature is repeated as recesses in the walls. The most noticeable features are the cool, two-tone green, decorative wall tiling and the black and white Italian mosaic flooring throughout.

You enter into an often crowded standing up area with a bar and hand carved oak panelling. Beyond is a sitting down and lunching area with a second bar and food servery which dispenses lunchtime sandwiches. Finally you come to the restaurant area with waitress service. The whole place has been beautifully preserved and it is very popular with a varied clientele ranging from lunchtime business people to shoppers and young people at weekends.

The choice and standard of food is excellent and deserving to be featured in the CAMRA Good Pub Food Guide. Lunchtime snacks consist of a wide choice of hot and cold filled sandwiches at £2 supplemented with bowls of chips. The restaurant section offers good quality Victorian Chop House style food with some imaginative touches averaging £5 − £7 for main courses. As you might expect the drinks are a little more expensive than other city centre pubs.

MANCHESTER CITY CENTRE
Peveril of the Peak

127 Great Bridgewater Street

Between Oxford and Lower Mosley Streets

Wilson's Bitter; Webster's Bitter; Ruddles Best Bitter, County

Closed Saturday until 7pm and Sunday

The **Peveril** is unchanging while everything around is transformed. Some years ago, after intervention by CAMRA and others, a new road scheme was made to go around the pub instead of ploughing through it, and now all the remaining surrounding buildings, in the heart of the Central Manchester Development Corporation Area, are gradually being demolished or revitalised. None of this disturbs

the relaxed informal atmosphere of the **Pev** however. It tends to be quiet most lunchtimes and in the evenings the trade ebbs and flows with the tide of nightlife from the numerous cinemas, theatres and clubs nearby.

The pub is about 170 years old but the wonderful green/gold Art Nouveau external tiling and the interior fittings date from around 1900. It is a listed building. Its unusual wedge shape results in similarly odd shaped rooms inside. There is an island bar contained inside some venerable mahogany and stained glass screens, and counters serving a drinking corridor and three small rooms: a public bar with an ancient open-topped table football machine which has been in place for at least 20 years; a cosy back parlour with an original Victorian fireplace and a further backroom which houses a juke box and pool table. In the summer months there is also provision for sitting outside.

As a city centre pub, it attracts quite a mixed clientele but with a high proportion of younger people. Lunchtime and early evening food is basic but good quality filled rolls and pies. During quiet lunchtimes, it is possible to take children into one of the rooms away from the bar. The pub is apparently named after a famous coach on the Manchester to London run. The coach driver is supposed to have profited so much from his journeys that he saved sufficient cash to buy the pub back in 1825.

MANCHESTER CITY CENTRE
Sinclair's Oyster Bar

Shambles Square

Behind Marks and Spencer which is at the corner of Corporation Street and Market Street

Samuel Smith Old Brewery Bitter, Museum Ale. (Also the complete range of Samuel Smith bottled products are available).

Sinclair's together with the **Old Wellington** next door are the last surviving timber framed structures in Manchester. They represent Manchester's token attempt to salvage a bit of its heritage from the comprehensive redevelopment of the area during the early 1970s.

Sinclair's Oyster Bar

To incorporate them into the shopping complex the buildings were raised a few feet. All traces of the surrounding environment in Market Place, where the Court Leet met and where criminals were publicly executed or punished in the stocks, have been obliterated.

The building was already old in 1738 when it opened as **John Shaws Punch House** and sometime in the 19th century it became **Sinclair's Oyster Rooms**. For three hundred years both buildings were owned by the Byrom family whose most famous member was John Byrom, the inventor of shorthand and the author of 'Christians Awake'.

Sinclair's was reopened as a pub on this site in 1981 by the Sam Smith brewery and, as they have done with many other historic pubs all over the country, they have restored the building and retained an air of antiquity with some sensitivity and care. The old beams look genuine and the low ceilings, extensive oak panelling, antique fireplaces and traditional pub furniture give the appropriate atmosphere. The walls and ceilings are decorated in ochres and browns to simulate old age and it works well. The pub is on two levels connected by a winding staircase and altogether there are about 8 different rooms and odd shaped alcoves giving some privacy and intimacy. There is a bar on each floor and a separate food servery downstairs.

Food is important but is not a dominant function of the pub. Available at lunchtimes only, the food catering offers a good choice of soups, roasts, home made pies, seafood and other traditional pub dishes including vegetarian options plus oysters of course. Main meals cost £3 to £4. If you just want a snack the upstairs bar offers soup, filled rolls, pork pie and ploughmans up to £2.50. There is an extensive wine list and tea and coffee are available. Beer prices are very reasonable for a central location like this. The pub is quite popular with younger people. Children are made welcome.

MANCHESTER CITY CENTRE

Unicorn Hotel

26 Church Street

Between High Street and Oldham Street

Bass Light, Draught Bass; Stones Bitter; Worthington Best Bitter

This is an up-market drinkers pub in the market area of town. It has no public bar or darts or dominoes or any of that but on the other hand there are no distractions to the business of drinking, such as food or juke boxes or televisions. What makes the place distinctive is the extensive use of oak in wall panelling, bar fittings, screens, doors and even cornices. There is also good use of stained glass including an unusual lighting panel in the ceiling. The interior looks as though it has been very well cared for since the 1930s. Around a centre bar there is a standing area, an L-shaped lounge and four separate little parlours radiating off, a couple with open fires. On the first floor there is a large function room.

The pub is the headquarters of the 'Honourable Order of Bass Drinkers' a sort of juvenile masonic lodge, who meet to 'organise regular cultural outings and soirees in order to enjoy the fine taste of the country's premier ale'. The pub has its regulars including the local market traders and also a mixture of shoppers and office workers. It is busy at lunchtime and quieter in the evenings. The pub is close to Manchester's main jazz venues. It is interesting to note that the **Unicorn** is excluded from 'Inns of the North', Bass's selective touring guide to northern inns — so it must be a good pub.

MIDDLETON

Old Boars Head

Long Street

A664, just north of town centre

Car parking in adjacent streets

Lees Mild, Bitter, Moonraker

This is the Lees Brewery flagship pub. Mostly 14th century and 12th century in parts, this famous half timbered Middleton landmark underwent an extensive restoration in 1988/89 and, despite spending around £$^1/_2$ million on it, the brewery resisted any temptation to relegate its pub function and turn it into a restaurant as has happened to other famous old inns. Also praiseworthy is the way in which the antiquity of the place has not been overwhelmed by modern finishes. The result is a pleasing blend of

genuinely old and reproduction old combined with the comfort and convenience of the 20th century.

There is a long central bar and eight separate rooms with varying floor levels, some away from the bar. There are five fireplaces with open fires and each room gives the visitor a different atmosphere. It is a pub to explore. One cosy little room has a Sam Bamford theme, celebrating Middleton's famous hand loom weaver turned radical author. Another room, the Sessions Room, was used as a court at one time and is like a Medieval banqueting room with a high ceiling and an enormous stone fireplace. Needless to say there are no juke boxes or fruit machines, just unobtrusive piped music.

The pub attracts a wide range of people of all ages. Children are allowed into the rooms which are away from the bar and in the summer months there is also a very pleasant beer garden at the rear of the pub. The lunchtime menu comprises soups, main dishes at around £3, including a vegetarian option, and sweets. Sandwiches are also available. The pub was deservedly awarded the 1991 Good Pub Guide 'Best Pub Restoration of the Year'.

MIDDLETON

Tandle Hill Tavern

14 Thornham Lane, Thornham Fold

On a dirt track between A664 and A671, OS reference
SD898091

Lees Mild, Bitter plus Moonraker (winter months)

Closed weekday lunchtimes, open 7.30pm evenings

You can drive to this pub along a dirt track but it is nicer to walk (or
ride). The Tandle Hill Country Park is nearby. Despite being no
more than a mile from the built up areas of Middleton and Royton,
the location is truly rural and the pub has a truly rural feel with
roaring fires in winter and some solid old furniture. It is clean,
comfortable, unpretentious and friendly and there are no juke

boxes or fruit machines. The building was probably a farmhouse at one time.

There is one large room with bar across a corner and separate tap room with a television and where you can take children at lunchtimes. Bar snacks are available – pie and peas and sandwiches with hot fillings, very reasonably priced. The pub keeps busy enough through the winter but probably the best time to go is during summer when you can sit outside and admire the extensive views of the moors above Rochdale. The pub is known colloquially as the **'Tanglehill Tavern'** and this has been etched into the glass of the inner door then noticeably altered to the correct spelling.

MOSSLEY

Colliers Arms

Broadcarr Lane

South of Mossley, east of A670 OS reference
SD962027

Bass Toby Light; Stones Bitter (both keg-not real ale)

Opening times are a bit erratic

This is a wonderfully unspoilt 18th century pub in the hills between
Oldham and Mossley, close by Hartshead Pike. Mind your head as
you enter the doorway and a little way down the corridor is a small
scullery-like room with a hatch. The beer is dispensed from here.
There were three public rooms at one time but one has been taken
over by the licensee as a living room – still with its bench seating
and Britannia tables – and at some time or other has been

converted into toilets at the behest of the Public Health authorities. The remaining room is low ceilinged with odd corners, ancient wallpaper and a piano. In summertime most visitors sit outside at the cobbled area in front of the pub or on the stone wall nearby.

Nothing has changed for donkey's years. The licensee is getting on a bit and is keeping the place ticking over but is patently not interested in any new fangled ideas such as serving food, allowing children in, or juke boxes, gambling machines or real ale. Some might find the place a bit dark and dingy but in fact it is a splendid living example of how pubs used to be. Hartshead Pike, 285 metres above sea level, was originally a Roman fire beacon site from which you can survey the four old counties of Lancashire, Yorkshire, Cheshire and Derbyshire. The whole area is criss-crossed with footpaths. If you want to know more you can purchase a sketch and potted history of this Lancashire landmark for £1 in the pub.

OLDHAM

Gardeners Arms

Mill Bottom, Waterhead

Two miles east of town centre, off A62, near junction of Broadoak Street and Dunham Street

Parking available on Medlock Valley car park adjacent to pub

Robinson's Best Mild, Best Bitter

The pub used to be on the main Oldham-Huddersfield Road but it is now by-passed by the main road and, although difficult to find, it is well worth seeking out. Situated next to a weir on the River Medlock, it was rebuilt in the late 1920s and there have been very few changes since then. The heart of the pub is the large central bar area with some nice features of the period — half height wall tiling with a black and gold frieze and leaded and coloured glass.

There is also much dark, moulded woodwork, attractive floor tiling, three original fireplaces and an extensive brass collection. Radiating off the central area there is a front games room, a back pool room and a large lounge/concert room running from front to back.

The **Gardeners** is a good community pub providing something for everyone – pub games, live music at weekends, in summer a pleasant beer garden next to the river and, on weekdays, a range of basic and cheap lunchtime meals and snacks. The pub is surrounded by a pleasant ,cleared grassy area on the banks of the River Medlock.

OLDHAM
Royal Oak

172 Manchester Road, Werneth

A62 approach to Oldham from Manchester

Parking in adjacent side streets

Robinson's Best Mild, Best Bitter

The **Royal Oak** is everything you would expect of a well run, traditional community pub. It has been with the same licensee since 1970 and it shows. It is a family-run pub with a relaxed and homely atmosphere and it attracts a good cross section of local people (young and old), who tend to keep to their own particular rooms. There are four rooms: an L-shaped lounge/bar area, and away from the bar a pool room, a games room and a separate, quieter lounge for conversation.

There have only been a few piecemeal alterations to the pub since it was first built in 1824. Some attractive wood panelling remains which, together with some basic comfortable furniture and great collection of jugs, plates, mirrors and brass and copperware, all contribute to the homeliness of the place. A potted history of the pub listing all its previous licensees is proudly displayed in the bar area. Too many traditional pubs like the **Royal Oak** have been lost to new road and redevelopment schemes in Oldham and it is still happening just to the north and south of Manchester Road, but miraculously this pub has survived.

OPENSHAW
Oddfellows Arms

12 Abbey Hey Lane

Just off and south of Ashton Old Road, A634

Street parking

Boddingtons Mild, Bitter

The **Oddfellows** is not as original as the **Hare and Hounds** q.v. just down the road in Gorton but it is in the same traditional mould and is as successful as a home-from-home community local. It is an interesting example of how to extend a pub and enhance its character rather than destroy it, as usually happens. Twelve years ago, it was a tiny two-roomed pub and it was enlarged by taking over the living quarters downstairs. The alteration is virtually seamless and the pub appears as an integral whole. The living quarters became the vault and it looks as though it has always been there. The original vault became the lounge and the bar parlour is now rechristened the smoke room. A couple of replacement windows have been etched in traditional fashion and all the original doors are in place.

New floor coverings and upholstery combine well with plain wooden fittings and there are some nice mirrors and naval memorabilia on the walls. There is a thriving social club which organises outings and occasional live entertainment and a collection of trophies for darts, cribbage and dominoes is proudly displayed in the vault. The **Oddfellows** is the only Boddington pub in the area which serves Boddingtons mild alongside the bitter.

PRESTWICH

Ostrich Hotel

163 Bury Old Road

A665 near A6044 junction, opposite Heaton Park

Forecourt parking

Holt Mild, Bitter

The name is derived from the family crest of the local landowning family, the Cokes. The present building dates from the 1880s and it replaced a 17th century farmhouse pub. The **Ostrich** is a great place to visit as an antidote to pub interior design schemes. It is the antithesis of interior design with fittings and decor as un-smart, un-coordinated and un-trendy as you are likely to find. The building itself has had bits added on and bits taken away now and then so there are different ceiling heights, different floor finishes and

various size doorways. This eclecticism is then compounded by the diverse collection of furnishings and light fittings and the overall result is a glorious jumble of styles and fashions from different ages.

There is a central bar with a corridor running alongside and no less than six different rooms. Some of the rooms are quite private and quiet, others have no doors and large rectangular apertures cut out of the walls so you are separate yet involved with the rest of the pub. One room is devoted to a pool table, another is for darts and another games. The lighting is not too bright, either from natural or artificial sources. As you can imagine, this uncontrived setting results in a very relaxed and homely atmosphere and scattered throughout its various places you will find young and old, couples, groups and a pleasant hum of conversation with minimal interference from the one fruit machine and old fashioned freestanding juke box. Food, in the form of filled rolls is usually available at all times.

ROCHDALE

Cemetery

470 Bury Road

B6222, corner of Sandy Lane, $^3/_4$ mile west of town centre

Small car park at rear

Boddingtons Bitter; Castle Eden Ale; Flowers Original

The pub appears to be rather ordinary from the outside but once past the threshold you will marvel at the classy and carefully preserved interior. It was built, soon after the cemetery was established in the 1860s, for the local Crown Brewery. The brewery was taken over in 1959 by Duttons of Blackburn and these days the beers come from the Whitbread stable but guest

beers also make an appearance. The most striking feature as you enter are the rich green/blue/gold tiles in the hall and bar lobby. Each room has an individual character and refurbishment works over the years have obviously nurtured these characteristics.

All three rooms are sited away from the bar. The front parlour is unusually shaped and abundant in mahogany with an impressive fireplace and privacy screens to give added intimacy. The rear snug is wedge-shaped with magnificent windows. The old vault is more basic with wood panelling, parquet floors and an old kitchen range. The lobby area around the bar is plain in comparison but good use is made of mirrors. Even the presence of a juke box and fruit machines in the hall cannot detract from the overall effect. Home cooked food is available lunchtimes. Children are welcome.

SALFORD

Braziers Arms

54 Hodson Street

Off Blackfriars Road, can be seen from Trinity Way

Parking in street

Boddingtons Mild, Bitter

The **Braziers** has evolved over the last 150 years or so out of three terraced houses and in many respects it is an archetypal, basic, back street local but there is also something special about it. It has not been messed about with too much and it has always been well run for the benefit of the locals. They are used to

strangers popping in though: groups of Manchester office workers, Boddingtons executives and simply people who appreciate a good traditional pub when they find one. The locals are friendly enough — perhaps too friendly. It helps if you go there when you have had a few.

After gently deteriorating for about 20 years the pub was recently repaired and refurbished in a way which retained all the best features such as the layout of vault, smoke room and bar parlour, the lobby area and the two hatches to the bar and a few original fixtures and fittings. It is a popular, busy pub full of local characters and be prepared for the competing noise from two televisions and a juke box which has a good selection of Irish songs. There is live music also from Thursday to Sunday evenings including sing-alongs and various groups.

SALFORD

Star

Back Hope Street

Off Bury New Road between Lower Broughton Road and Great Clowes Street

Street parking nearby

Robinson's Best Mild, Best Bitter, Old Tom (winter only)

The **Star** is a bit of an institution in this part of Salford. It is an odd pub, verging on the idiosyncratic and perhaps reflecting the character of the area. It is well known to generations of students who have lived in lodgings close by. This area of Broughton, known as the Cliff, is rich in history and is a Conservation Area. Some of the grandest and oldest houses in Salford are to be found here, built for the wealthy merchants of the 19th century. Close by there are pleasant walks down to the banks of the River Irwell and along the Croal-Irwell valley trail. Also close by are areas of inner city blight and dereliction which tend to encroach.

You are served from a tiny public bar, the cosiest part of the pub but usually occupied by regulars. The rest of the pub consists of a simply furnished lounge, or, in summer, a sheltered beer garden which is basically the yard of the pub. The **Star** has been run by the same family for over 20 years and as a result it has that feeling of continuity and stability. It has the curious distinction of having an inside Gents' toilet and an outside Ladies'. The beer garden is OK for children in the summer. There is no food available. On Wednesday evenings there is a popular folk club, the oldest in Salford.

WHITEFIELD
Coach and Horses

71 Bury Old Road

A665 near Besses o' th' Barn BR Station

Parking on forecourt

Holt Mild, Bitter

Visiting this pub is like communing with another age. It is an old coaching inn dating from 1830, still with an attached stable block and in the early days it had its own brewhouse. It was once a staging post for the Manchester to Burnley mail coach and is still

used by today's postman! The sort of pub which attracts loyal regulars and long term licensees, it has featured in the Good Beer Guide for 14 years.

The wide entrance hall leads straight to the bar and the three rooms, vault, lounge and snug are all located away from the bar. There is nothing special about the building except its continuity with the past and virtually unchanged layout for 160 years. There are very few pubs which can make the same boast. The addition of a bay window to the lounge is the only significant alteration. In the good weather you may sit outside. There is no juke box or fruit machines and there is no call for food so eat elsewhere.

SOME FURTHER SUGGESTIONS

Blue Bell, Robinson's
13 Market Street, Shaw (north of Oldham, off A663)

Britannia, Lees
2 Rowsley Street, Beswick (east of Manchester city centre, off A662)

Buck and Hawthorne, Robinson's
Katherine Street, Ashton-under-Lyne (off A627, west of town centre)

Castle Hotel, Robinson's
66 Oldham Street (Manchester city centre)

Clockface, Tetley
Old Hall Street, Kearsley (south of Bolton, near junction of A666 and A5082)

Cross Keys, Vaux
95 Jersey Street, Ancoats (north of Manchester city centre, off A665)

Concert, Boddingtons
13 Fairfield Road, Openshaw (off A635)

Farmers Arms, Lees
Simister Lane, Simister (remote village, best approached from A665, Prestwich)

Friendship Tavern, Marston's
786 Hyde Road, Gorton (A57)

Globe, Boddingtons
Whitworth Road, Rochdale (A671, just outside the town centre)

Kings Head, Walker
Junction Road, Deane, Bolton (western outskirts, off A676)

Lord Nelson, Thwaites
Kearsley Hall Road, Ringley, Kearsley (south of Bolton, off A667)

Mawson Hotel, Tetley
78 Francis Street (off Brunswick Street) Chorlton-on-Medlock
(south of Manchester city centre, off A34)

Moulders Arms, Burtonwood
Heyrod Street (off Adair Street), Ancoats (east of Manchester city
centre, off Great Ancoats Street)

Old Dun Horse, Thwaites
Bolton Street, Ramsbottom (north of Bury, A676)

Old Post Office, Oldham,Chesters
439 Manchester Road, Hollinwood (south of Oldham, A62)

Plough Hotel, Robinson's
Hyde Road, Gorton (corner Wellington Street, A57)

Royal Oak, Robinson's
178 Union Street, Oldham (town centre)

Smith's Arms, Burtonwood
Sherratt Street, Ancoats (off A62)

Smithfield, Boddingtons
1062 Ashton Old Road, Openshaw (A635)

Welcome, Holt
53 Bury Old Road, Whitefield (A665)

White Lion, Whitbread
6 Bolton Street, Bury (town centre)

Wrexham, Burtonwood
1174 Ashton Old Road, Openshaw (A635)

Ye Olde Nelson, Whitbread
285 Chapel Street, Salford (A6)

In the Manchester area, a number of pubs have been saved from closure or unsympathetic refurbishment in recent years thanks to some vigorous campaigning by CAMRA and other local groups. The general climate of opinion is slowly shifting to view the loss of our traditional pubs as 'a bad thing', but it is a continual battle against the breweries, local authority engineers and planners, and a general tendency to sweep away anything which is distinctive or unusual, simply because it is old or does not fit in with the over-riding commercial ethic.

The **Old Post Office**, Hollinwood, is a characterful, basic and unspoilt ex-**Oldham Brewery** pub which was indeed a post office in earlier years. It has about 12 months of life before the Manchester Outer Ring Road ploughs through it. Visit it while you can.

Ye Olde Nelson in Salford is also threatened by a road scheme, or rather one metre or so of the front of the building is in the way of a road widening scheme for the A6 and, rather than compromise their wonderful design standards for dual carriageway highways, the city engineers intend to destroy the whole pub. It dates from 1897 and both internally and externally it is a very well preserved pub and well worth a visit while it still stands.

In Manchester the city planners have attempted to have regard for pubs in their Hyde Road widening scheme and there is still a chance that the **Plough**, Gorton, dating from 1823, may be granted lease of life. Because the pub has been blighted by the scheme for more than a decade the brewery has not been inclined to mess about with it and it has retained its original multi room plan form and some fine architectural features including a beautiful carved back bar fitting.

On the fringe of central Manchester the wonderful **Britannia**, Beswick, has managed to cling on and prosper in its back street, backwater location while all around has been transformed into an inner city wasteland. It is a popular pub with some attractive traditional features, situated right on the boundary of the proposed Eastlands Olympic Stadium.

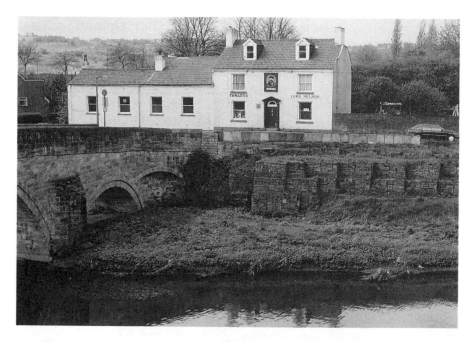

A different kind of calamity threatens the **Lord Nelson** at Ringley. It is a nice old pub in a picturesque location with a good traditional layout of small bar and four rooms off a central corridor and has not been interfered with for many years. However, Thwaites now want to open up the interior and make it indistinguishable from thousands of others. The best time to visit is soon, before it changes, on a summer Sunday lunchtime when you can lunch in the beer garden and walk by the River Irwell close by.

Pubs in Manchester city centre have gradually been gentrified during the past 20 years and the more basic 'local' type pubs which serve mild and provide cheap snacks and a more homely ambience are thin on the ground. The **Castle** fulfils this role admirably. It is a 200 year old listed building, the only Robinsons outlet in the city centre, serving all four Robinson beers at reasonable prices.

On the fringes of the city centre the **Cross Keys**, **Smiths Arms**, **Moulders Arms** in Ancoats are all good traditional pubs with unspoilt, multi-roomed interiors which have managed to survive in an unpromising environment. The **Smiths** is the oldest pub in the area. The interior was refitted in basic style in the 1930s and it is largely unaltered, the vault especially.

The **Cross Keys** was given a rare CAMRA 'Traditional Pub Award' in 1987 and it is still as deserving. The **Moulders** has a beautiful tiled exterior and a plain but interesting interior of small rooms and narrow passageways which give the pub some intimacy and character. Irish music is performed Saturday and Sunday nights.

In Chorlton-on-Medlock, near the University, the **Mawson** is another pub which has survived while streets of terraced housing around have been demolished. Again, a multiroom pub of 1930s provenance with some 1980s refurbishment which, if anything, has enhanced its appeal.

If you find yourself in the Gorton/Openshaw area, perhaps visiting the **Hare and Hounds q.v.** and **Oddfellows Arms q.v.**, it is worth while taking in the rest of a small cluster of relatively unspoilt Boddington pubs nearby. The **Concert** was recently rescued from a very run down state without being turned into a plastic palace. It has become a basic and plain but comfortable back street local.

Similarly, the **Wrexham** (recently sold to a new pub-owning group) is a thriving little pub with three rooms and some excellent tiling and cut glass and the **Smithfield**, although subject to recent alterations and refurbishment, has retained three rooms and some good 1930s features including excellent and extensive wall tiling in unusual Art Deco geometric patterns.

Around and about Manchester it is worth a visit to the **Blue Bell**, Shaw, an unusual pub of 18th century origin whose original brewhouse room behind the bar has been incorporated into the pub. The interior was re-modeled in the 1900s and there have been few structural changes since then. One nice feature is the Arts and Crafts style inglenook in the old tap room.

In Ashton, the **Buck and Hawthorn** has recently had the treatment from Robinsons Brewery. Some parts of the pub were improved but it lost a particularly nice glazed screen from the back of the main room. However, it is still an interesting multi-roomed pub with a tiny bagatelle-shaped snug and many interior features dating from the 1920s.

While in the vicinity of the **Lord Nelson**, mentioned above, it is worth visiting the **Clockface** in Farnworth. The Manchester

'Vintage Pubs' guide (1988) described this pub as 'a friendly, three-roomed, unaltered, softly lit, no frills, back street, community pub with a large vault and a superb gents toilet'. It is still the same.

If you manage to visit the **Plough**, mentioned above, it is only a short distance to the **Friendship** which is another unspoilt 1930s pub, rather shabby and, despite its name, not very friendly but a good example of a genre which has almost disappeared. There are three rooms and some nice features including marquetry panelling.

Simister, which still has a village feel to it, is the sort of place where you would expect to find a good traditional pub. The **Farmers Arms** is a very old building which became a pub in 1727. It has a well preserved rustic atmosphere with a mixture of real and false beams.

Tetley Walker have recently taken over a historic pub on the outskirts of Bolton. The **Kings Head**, a listed building in a Conservation Area, has been re-Victorianised quite successfully and now has landscaped car-parks, beer garden, an extensive food menu and all mod cons.

Ramsbottom receives more visitors these days with the advent of the East Lancashire Railway. Visitors could do worse than to wend their way up the main street to the **Old Dun Horse**, another 1930s pub originally of the Bury Brewery. It is a large, airy, high ceilinged pub with four rooms and the best feature is the attractive and extensive wall tiling of the period.

The **Royal Oak** in Oldham **q.v.** has a sister **Royal Oak** in the town centre and, just to add to the confusion, it belongs to the same brewery, Robinsons. The best room is the tiny snug at the front of the building with a hatch to the bar — presumably an outdoor (off sales) department at one time. The original, shuttered, quadrant-shaped bar is another good feature.

From the centre of Oldham to the centre of Bury. The **White Lion** is reminiscent of an Edwardian Holts pub. It still has revolving doors, much mahogany fitting out and ornate ceilings. The best part is the Oak Room at the rear of the pub with its full height oak panels and carved oak fireplace. The room is used as a television and darts room and also as a clubroom for the 'Submarine' and 'HMS Illustrious' Old Comrades Associations. There is much naval memorabilia on the walls.

The **Globe** in Rochdale is similar to the **White Lion** in many ways but more impressive. The original layout of four rooms is still intact

and so is the original Edwardian mahogony panelling, tiling, decorative glass and plasterwork. It is slightly shabby and noisy at times but well worth a visit.

Finally, a suggestion for a mini pub crawl of three architecturally contrasting Holt pubs in Whitefield and Prestwich: the **Coach and Horses q.v.**, with its unaltered 160 year old plan form; the **Ostrich q.v.**, with its characterful jumble of styles; and the **Welcome**, built in 1936 in distinctive interwar style and, although it has recently had the interior designer treatment, its basic fabric is virtually unaltered and indeed the oak panelling and bar and fireplaces have been enhanced.

Manchester and Salford Freehouses

Beerhouse 5 Angel Street, Manchester city centre, (just off Rochdale Road, Close to Miller Street and inner relief route)

Crescent 18 The Crescent, Salford (A6, opposite Salford University)

Dock and Pulpit Encombe Place, Salford (off Chapel Street, A6, behind Salford Royal Hospital)

Kings Arms Hotel 4A Helmshore Walk, Chorlton-on-Medlock (off Skerry Close, off Wadeson Road, off Brunswick Street)

Kings Arms Ale House Bloom Street, Salford (off Chapel Street, A6, close to intersection with inner relief route)

Marble Arch 73 Rochdale Road, Collyhurst (junction with Gould Street, just up from Beerhouse)

Queens Arms 6 Honey Street, Cheetham (off Redbank, off Cheetham Hill Road, A665)

White House 122 Great Ancoats Street, Ancoats (A665, opposite Central Retail Park)

Mancunians are fortunate in having a number of proper free houses, free to serve any range of beers, dotted around the fringe of the central business area. They have all sprung up in recent years, invariably in pubs which had been abandoned by the big brewers because they were considered to be uneconomic. The **Marble Arch** in 1984, the **Crescent** in 1986 and the Queens Arms in 1987 were all created by entrepreneurial local CAMRA members and the **White House** (1985) and the **Beerhouse** (1987) were started along similar lines. The **Kings Arms Ale House** is owned by the Boddington Pub Company and has been run as a freehouse since 1990. The **Dock and Pulpit** is a very recent venture by the owners of the **Crescent**. The **Kings Arms** is actually a brew pub but with a wide range of excellent beers.

The **Marble Arch** is the most interesting building. Listed, grade II, it was built in 1888 in the style of a London pub with walls and a high barrel-vaulted ceiling of glazed brick and a sloping mosaic floor, presumably all designed to be easily hosed down after a hectic Saturday night. There are two rooms, each with its own bar and usually at least half a dozen regularly changing beers on offer

plus traditional cider. The quality of the food has earned it a place in the CAMRA Good Pub Food Guide (hot food available all day) and there is live music several nights of the week.

A short walk across the River Irk brings you to the **Queens Arms**, a thriving pub, recently doubled in size to be able to accommodate its enthusiastic customers. One reason for its popularity is the range of beers including the distinctive and well made **Bateman** beers, carted all the way from Lincolnshire. **Taylor Landlord** is another regular and there are usually five guest beers in addition plus a good selection of foreign bottled beers. This pub is also in the CAMRA Good Pub Food Guide where it is singled out for its multi cultural dishes and reasonable prices. In summer the beer garden at the rear gives you a splendid view of the Irk Valley industrial landscape and the railway sidings.

The **Crescent** is a rambling and rather derelict but characterful pub, popular with students and staff at nearby Salford University. **Holt** beers are the regulars and there are usually at least three or

four guest beers in addition and the occasional traditional cider. There are three rooms plus overspill areas, a few cats and welcoming open fires in winter.

The **Beerhouse** is exactly what it says: a two-roomed, basic, utilitarian watering hole boasting 18 handpumps which dispense **Thwaites, Holt and Dobbin's bitters** plus many guest beers including Belgian beers on draught and over 100 foreign bottled beers.

The **Kings Arms Ale House** began as an experiment by the Boddington Pub Company and it has turned out a success. Regular beers include **Theakston, Taylor, Batham, Holt** plus guest beers and traditional ciders. There is a large, unusually-shaped room with some good original features and a small snug off the corridor. Blues music night is on alternate Sundays.

The **Dock and Pulpit**, about midway between the **Crescent** and the **Kings Arms Ale House**, is a small pub due to open Autumn 1992 after being closed for years. The beers here come from the **Scottish and Newcastle** stable plus **Tetley** and **Marston's** plus regularly changing guest beers.

The **White House** is a two room pub which limits itself to three or four well kept beers including **Holt Bitter**.

The other **Kings Arms** is rather difficult to find, being situated in the middle of an unprepossessing residential estate but it is worth making the effort, both for the quality of its beer, brewed on the premises, and because it has become a thriving and vibrant pub with four regular real ales plus real ciders and a ginger beer! and a range of foreign bottled beers. Live music is another attraction on Mondays, Tuesdays and Thursdays. (See the section on Lancashire breweries also).

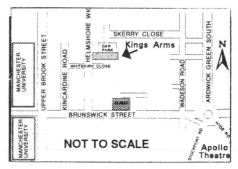

Liverpool and South Lancashire

AUGHTON

Dog and Gun Inn

Long Lane

Between Aughton and Ormskirk, near Aughton Park BR
Station, off A59

Car park at rear

Burtonwood Mild, Bitter, Foreshaw's Bitter

Closed lunchtimes Monday to Friday

This is a superb little local; well preserved, comfortable and with a
good community atmosphere. The bowling club is the centre of
activity and the bowling green at the rear is a pleasant haven
surrounded by gardens, a perfect setting for supping Foreshaws
on a warm summer evening.

Originally the pub was a rural tavern with a smallholding before the
area was built up. Around the turn of the century it was owned by
the Knowles Brewery of Ormskirk and about this time it must have
acquired its distinctive facade and internal fittings. A few years ago
the entrance and lobby area was opened out a little but the
alterations are not noticeable. On each side of the lobby and bar
are two comfortable rooms with real coal fires. The pub is quite

unspoilt and home-
spun with wood
grained finishes and
traditional style furni-
ture. Its location on
the edge of town in a
residential area
means that it is
mainly used by local
people.

HASKAYNE

Kings Arms

Delf Lane

A567 between Maghull and Southport

Forecourt parking

Tetley, Mild, Bitter; Cains Bitter; one other regular guest beer

Reputed to date from 1823, the **Kings Arms** became a brewpub sometime during the 19th century and supplied other local pubs around. There have been very few changes to the pub during this century. It still has its three downstairs rooms, now augmented by a games room and there are some attractive traditional features such as the leaded and stained glass windows, grained woodwork, parquet flooring and a couple of fine fireplaces. There are five working fireplaces altogether, usually burning logs in wintertime.

The place is decorated with some rare old Tetley mirrors and portraits and other memorabilia of all the English monarchs.

The pub is run in a very friendly and efficient manner, catering for locals and visitors. Daily newspapers are supplied for the customers and there is quite an extensive catering operation but it is based on the first floor and this results in a successful combination of both restaurant and pub which do not impinge on each other. At lunchtimes (except Tuesdays) a range of starters (£1 to £2), salads (£3), main meals (£3 to £4) and sandwiches are available at the bar or in the restaurant. There are always daily specials, a vegetarian choice and children's meals. The evening menu is a bit more upmarket with casseroles, fish dishes and vegetarian meals around £5 to £6 and various steak dishes at £7 to £10. In addition there are homemade desserts, coffees with liqueurs and a basic wine list. The evening menu is available in the restaurant from Thursday to Sunday evenings.

As you enter the pub there are two small parlours to the right with a hatch to the bar. The public bar and the games room are to the left. The games room has a juke box but the remainder of the pub is quiet. At the side of the pub the old stables and cobbled yard make an attractive beer garden. While in the vicinity you can take a stroll along the towpath of the Leeds-Liverpool Canal which is situated a few yards away.

LATHOM

Railway Tavern

Station Road, Hoscar Moss

$3/_4$ mile north of A5209, OS reference SD 469116 (next to Hoscar Station)

Own car park

Tetley Mild, Bitter; Jennings Bitter

'Unspoilt and homely' sums up this place. It is quite an old building which received a comprehensive fitting out a few decades ago and has been cared for and not messed about with ever since. It is amazing how the five separate spaces and three bar counters could be fitted into such a small building. This is achieved by a layout of small inter-connecting rooms around a central bar. There is much solid wood in the bar fittings, bench seating and bric-a-brac shelves. Juke box and pool table are noticeably absent and there is a real coal fire in winter.

About 20 years ago, for some reason, the stars of Coronation Street came to this part of deepest Lancashire and visited the pub and a photograph of the visit has pride of place on the wall. The

atmosphere is relaxed and friendly. Good value, genuine home cooked food is available lunchtimes and evenings and children are welcome. Built into the front wall of the pub there is a rare Victorian post box.

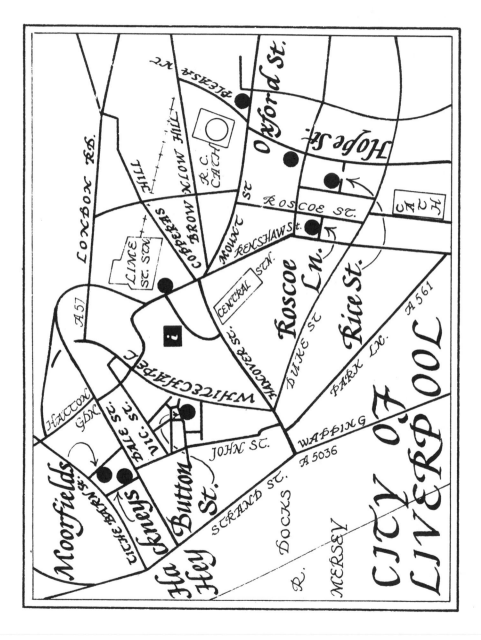

LIVERPOOL CITY CENTRE

Lion Tavern

67 Moorfields

Corner of Tythbarn Street, opposite former Exchange Station site

Ind Coope Burton Ale; Walker Mild, Bitter (and Walker Winter Warmer in season)

The pub closes all day Sunday

There are grander and more ornate Victorian pubs in Liverpool but the **Lion** manages to be architecturally impressive and at the same time familiar and welcoming. There is a friendly atmosphere and the beer and food is reasonably priced so it attracts a wide range of customers. The Victorian splendour lies in the ornate details of the carved woodwork, rich tiling and mirror and cut glass, the high ceilings and fine fireplaces and in one backroom a wonderful coloured glass domed skylight.

There are three rooms (smoke room/public bar and two parlours) plus space around the screened bar and at lunchtimes the whole pub can be busy with businessmen and regulars who come for the bargain lunches. The pub is named after the Lion locomotive which pulled one of the first trains between Manchester and Liverpool's Exchange Station. It is a listed building.

Interior scenes from The Lion Tavern

LIVERPOOL CITY CENTRE

Oxford

67 Oxford Street

Corner of Florist Street, near Grove Street

Higsons Bitter; Cains Bitter

The **Oxford** is a survivor. All the surrounding property was demolished long ago leaving the pub as a reminder of the bustle and activity that used to be. Today it is mainly frequented by students and teachers from the University nearby. It is a homely, basic pub, in many ways indistinguishable from hundreds of others if it were not for the convivial atmosphere generated by the

combination of caring licensee and the lively clientele. Changes have been minimal and thankfully there has been no attempt by the brewery to rationalise the layout. Much of the front room is taken up by the bar. In the back room there is room for a few tables and chairs and there is an open fire in winter.

It is usually a loud and cheerful place with a television and music competing with student chatter. The pub is much appreciated for its food; a variety of snacks up to £2, and a different main dish each day for £2.50. A three course Sunday lunch is a speciality, £4.50.

LIVERPOOL CITY CENTRE
Philharmonic Hotel

36 Hope Street

Corner of Hardman Street, opposite Philharmonic Hall and near the Roman Catholic Cathedral

Tetley, Mild, Bitter; Cains Bitter; Jennings Bitter; Ind Coope Burton Ale

Liverpool can boast of having two of the most splendid pub interiors in the whole of England in the **Philharmonic** and the **Vines**. The Philharmonic was built as a prestige house for the Robert Cain Brewery in 1900. No expense was spared, employing the finest designers and artists and craftsmen from the shipyards which had fitted out transatlantic liners. The listed building schedule describes the pub architecturally as 'exuberant free style'. The Art Nouveau wrought iron gates on the Hope Street entrance incorporates the brewery motto 'Pacem Amo'.

Views of the Philharmonic

Inside you are greeted with a visual feast of mosaic, ceramic, marble, mahogany, copper, brass, stained and cut glass and elaborate plasterwork. The overall effect is a richness of colour and detail which induces some awe and reverence in the first time beholder. It is not possible to give an adequate description here; it just has to be seen and experienced. And despite its grandeur, this being Liverpool, it is not a stuffy, unapproachable pub. The bar staff are friendly and you will come across all types here. If you look affluent you may be tapped for a drink by a Liverpool character. There is plenty of room and even at peak periods you can find a quiet corner in the public bar or one of the smaller snugs away from the main bar. Do not leave without seeing the Grand Lounge (ex-billiard room) with its sculptured naked women supporting the ceiling and its enormous chandeliers and, if you are able to, see the Gents' toilet, renowned as a cathedral among Gents'.

Lunchtime food is available every day, including Sunday, in the dining area upstairs which is 1971 'Victorian-style' provenance. Starters cost up to £1.40 and main meals, including salads, fish and vegetarian options, range from £2 to £3.25. There is also a range of sweets and tea and coffee is available.

LIVERPOOL CITY CENTRE

Roscoe Head

24 Roscoe Street

Off Leece Street, between city centre and the two cathedrals

Tetley Mild, Bitter; Jennings Bitter; Ind Coope Burton Ale

This is a popular little pub which has everything you might expect of a traditional back street city centre local: it is unaltered, it has no pool table, juke box or fruit machines, there are two open fires and the place is homely and comfortable. There is nothing special about the decor or the fixtures but the very convivial atmosphere derives from the intimacy of its small rooms and the people who use the pub – all sections of the community including local students. It was the 1991 local CAMRA Pub of the Year.

You have the choice of a tiny front snug separated from a standing up lobby area by leaded glass partitions, a front room away from the bar or a back lounge with a television. Good use of mirrors makes the pub seem larger than it is but in fact it can appear busy when there are only a few customers. It is evident that the brewery and successive licensees have not felt the need to alter anything for many years because the pub is wonderfully successful as it is. Long may it remain so. There is an extensive collection of ties in the back lounge (191 at the last count). Lunches are available, Monday to Saturday, comprising sandwiches, ploughmans, pizzas, hamburgers, curries, fish and their famous omelettes, all at prices ranging between £1.50 and £1.80. You cannot complain at that!

LIVERPOOL CITY CENTRE

Vines

81 Lime Street

Very handy for Lime Street BR Station

Walker Mild, Bitter, Best Bitter. (Foreign bottled beers also available)

Liverpool's other famous decorative pub was re-built in 1907 on the site of a previous pub dating from 1813. It was conceived by the same architect as the **Philharmonic** but unfortunately, the brewery management have seen fit to 'improve' on his original vision. In 1989, various alterations were carried out which altered the bar area, removed a small parlour and an original Edwardian WC and prettified the place a bit. Nevertheless the **Vines** or the **'Big House'** as it is known locally is still an impressive part of the Liverpool pub scene.

The Edwardian Baroque exterior of carved stone and marble gives an indication of the grandeur inside. The style is not quite as exuberant as the **Philharmonic**. It is slightly more sedate with

greater use of carved mahogany, oak panelling and cut glass. The ceilings and friezes are more ornate, there are magnificent fireplaces, enormous oil paintings and chandeliers and much polished copperwork and the spectacular glazed cupola in the 'heritage suite' (ex-billiard room) is a sight not to be missed. There are also modern carpets and brasswork and twee matching curtains and ceiling decor in 1990s style but this does not detract from the overall splendour. The name simply comes from a Mr Vines who owned the original pub on the site. Food is typical pub fare, reasonably priced at around £2 for a main course. Meals are usually available at most times of day.

LIVERPOOL CITY CENTRE
White Star

Button Street

Just off Matthew Street, the Beatle tourist trap

Stones Bitter; Worthington Best Bitter; Draught Bass (plus the remainder of the Bass range in keg form)

This is a proper boozer's local in the heart of the city, a cheerful friendly pub and, although there have been a succession of small changes over the years, the basic layout remains unaltered. Much mahogany and etched glass is in evidence and the real character

of the place has not been submerged. The **White Star** is a shrine for Bass drinkers almost on a par with the **Unicorn** in Manchester.

It has the look of a well used pub; it is usually busy and is becoming just a little worn around the edges. The public bar at the front has an attractive curved bar and opposite this, beneath the front windows, there is a partially screened snug area. At the rear is a further room, at one time a dining room but these days, being primarily a beer pub, it is not used as such. Fresh baked pies and rolls are usually available at all times. All around the pub there is White Star line memorabilia and a nice touch in the dining room is a rack of daily newspapers.

LIVERPOOL CITY CENTRE

Ye Cracke

13 Rice Street

Between Hope Street and Pilgrim Street in the shadow of the Anglican Cathedral

Oak Best Bitter; Marston Pedigree; plus guest beers

Originally the **Ruthin Castle**, the pub became known as **Ye Cracke** because the small bar parlour was so often crowded.

It has expanded since then and is now an original, vibrant pub with an atmosphere all of its own. Rice Street is now going up market with its new city centre town houses but the pub will no doubt

endure as the haunt of polytechnic students, artists, musicians and beer lovers. The interior, almost devoid of natural lighting, is uncarpeted and divided, in a haphazard way, into a variety of drinking areas. There is still a tiny bar parlour, a small back room, a 'war office', a central standing up area in front of the bar and a large room with an original 'Fiesta' juke box. The 'war office' is a small snug which has had its title since the Boer War. Local amateur military strategists would gather here to discourse and argue about the conduct of the war and the snug has borne the name ever since.

The pub is furnished with a good collection of benches, pews and Britannia tables and there are many framed pen and ink drawings of contemporary Liverpool. Out at the back is a small beer garden, rare for the city centre. It is the only city centre pub where children are more likely to be tolerated (but it is always advisable to ask first). The home cooked food is renowned for its excellent value and there is usually a vegetarian option. The regular beers are augmented by one or two guest beers, often from the Oak Brewery.

LIVERPOOL CITY CENTRE

Ye Hole in ye Wall

4 Hackins Hey

Between Tythbarn Street and Dale Street

Tetley Mild, Bitter; Draught Bass

Closed evenings, Monday to Thursday and Sunday

A very atmospheric pub established in 1726 on the site of a Quaker meeting house, this is probably the oldest pub in Liverpool. It was reputedly the haunt of sailors originally and it retains links with the sea these days as a shipping and insurance city gents pub. It is slightly below street level, with a minimum of natural light

and so gives the feeling of a hole-in-the-wall haven, insulated from the outside world. There is much stately dark oak panelling, dark wallpapers, dark leather upholstery and brass and copperware creating a gentlemen's club atmosphere. There is a standing up drinking area around the bar. A central chimney breast divides the rest of the pub into two main areas and the judicious use of oak partitions and screens create some cosy nooks and crannies. Obviously in this type of establishment there are no vulgar fruit machines and the juke box plays 50's and 60's music on free play at a sensible volume.

It is a place for informal business meetings and the swopping of city gossip. Although the bar proclaims Walkers and Burton cask ales, in fact the pub was acquired some years ago by Bellhaven Inns and the beers have changed. The beer dispense system is an unusual gravity dispense from the first floor 'cellar' through large oak pillars at either end of the bar. The lunchtime food menu gives a sensibly limited but well prepared selection of standard pub fare such as steak and kidney pie, curry and sandwiches. Food is not available on Saturdays.

LYDIATE

Scotch Piper

347 Southport Road

Lydiate is 8 miles north of Liverpool and the pub is about one mile north of the town centre on the A567

Own car park

Burtonwood Bitter

Dating from 1320 AD and reputed to be the oldest pub in Lancashire, the **Scotch Piper** is a picture postcard type pub with thatched roof and flower baskets hanging on its whitewashed, buttressed walls. the story goes that a long time ago it was called the **Royal Oak** and in fact was originally built around an oak tree which was used as a main support. During the Jacobite uprising of 1745 one of Bonnie Prince Charlie's highland pipers was brought,

wounded, to the inn and he recovered and married the landlord's daughter and that is how the pub received its name. The Moorcroft family had a connection with the pub for 500 years until 1945 when it was bought by Burtonwood Brewery.

There are three small rooms. To the far right, along a corridor there is a fairly comfortably furnished room with a carpet. The two other rooms are more basic with stone flagged floors, some simple bench seating and cosy open fires in winter. In summer you may prefer to sit at the tables and benches on the forecourt.

The pub is a listed building and it won a prestigious award from CAMRA's Pub Preservation Group in 1986. The brewery certainly deserved recognition for their careful, sympathetic scheme which has preserved the rustic simplicity of the building, respected its antiquity and, at the same time, introduced 20th century standards of cleanliness and comfort. There is no cellar and no bar counter. Instead, the beer is served from a tiny servery where the casks are stillaged and the beer is drawn off directly. Food is not available because there are no proper facilities for food catering. The pub has recently been sold to a pub retailing group which may affect the way it is run.

ORMSKIRK

Buck i' th' Vine Inn

35 Burscough Street

Pedestrianised area of town centre

__Walker Mild, Bitter__

The **Buck i' th' Vine** is a listed building, a historic coaching inn whose antecedents go back to 1650 but whose main fabric dates from the early 18th century. It still has an 'olde worlde' feel to it despite being regularly meddled with by the brewery. The most interesting part of the interior is the bar front with its ancient, curved 'sweetshop window', which you have to stoop under to place your order, and the cosy parlour at the back of the bar. Small private parlours behind the bar were once a feature of many northern pubs and to be invited in by the landlord was a social privilege. The parlour is the quietest part of the pub and it has a very traditional feel to it with leather seats and a fine, copper ornamented fireplace.

The central corridor was an open alleyway at one time, now roofed over. Off the corridor there are three further rooms which have been opened up to some extent. Opposite the bar, down two steps, there is a smoke room, traditionally furnished, including another distinctive fireplace and decorated with interior design artifacts. At the rear of the pub is a large lounge and a smaller darts and television room.

Full use is made of the outside area. The narrow pedestrianised street opens out onto a cobbled forecourt where tables and benches are provided and the eating and drinking is fully integrated into the street scene. There is another pleasant quiet sitting out area in the rear yard where you are surrounded by the old stalls and the original brewhouse of the pub. A good choice of reasonably priced snacks and meals are available at lunchtimes.

ORMSKIRK

Greyhound

100 Aughton Street

Southern approach to town centre, off A59

Public car parks nearby

Walker Mild, Bitter, Winter Warmer (in season)

The **Greyhound** is less trendy and more down-to-earth than the **Buck i' th' Vine**. Another old coaching inn, it is a long rambling pub with five contrasting rooms and a beer garden at the rear. These days its role is as a market town local and it attracts a good cross section of customers of all ages and both sexes.

The small front public bar is the least altered part of the pub and always the most crowded. The main bar is in the central lounge area which has an attractive carved wooden fireplace and panelled ceiling. Right at the back of the pub, up two steps, is a television and darts room, a small haven detached from the busy areas. Most of the pub is homely and unpretentious with wood graining and decor of various shades of brown and just the right level of lighting but two front rooms on the right have been prettified a bit with fancy wallpapers and pictures with spotlights. Bar snacks are available at lunchtimes.

PEMBERTON

Dog and Partridge

30 Chapel Street

Just off Ormskirk Road, A577, south of Wigan and half mile east of Junction 26, M6

Own car park

Greenalls Mild, Bitter

If you are asking for directions to this pub in Pemberton ask for **'Jem Lowes'** rather than **Dog and Partridge**. The pub was run by the Lowe family for 47 years and the old nickname has stuck. The pub is an original little gem. It was probably a beerhouse at one time and the 1829 datestone on the gable gives an indication of its antiquity. Pubs like this are very rare these days. What makes it special is its unspoilt qualities – unchanged for decades, just

gradually adapting to changing requirements over the years and devoid of any purpose made pub fittings so it has a homely, domestic feel.

When you enter you have to go hunting for the bar which is through a narrow corridor and down two steps to a back room. This is the heart of the pub and the busiest area. Off the corridor on one side there is an L-shaped lounge area with television, juke box and piano and on the other side a small parlour with well worn domino tables and saucy calendars on the walls. All sections of the local community enjoy the pub like a home from home. It is in the heart of rugby league country and the walls of the lounge are covered with photos of teams from the 1930s to the 1960s. The locals, of course, just take their pub for granted and do not expect visitors from outside the area but as long as you do not look as though you are from 'The Social', you will be OK.

SKARISBRICK

Heatons Bridge Inn

2 Heatons Bridge

B5242, north of Ormskirk, OS reference SD 404118.

Forecourt parking

Tetley Mild, Bitter

This is one of the many canal-side pubs along this section of the Leeds-Liverpool Canal. The datestone above the door shows that the building dates from 1837. It is typical of the cottage style of buildings around this part of the Lancashire Plain. It has not been spoiled by too many changes. There are a couple of drinking spaces adjacent to the bar and a separate vault and a 'doubles' room away from the bar, all with low ceilings and just the right amount of lighting to enhance the cosy and intimate atmosphere.

There are no noisy fruit machines or juke boxes and in winter there are real coal fires. All sorts of unusual bric-a-brac decorate the

walls which makes a change from the usual brewery job lot. By the bar there is a ships bell with a notice 'Whoever rings this bell in jest will buy a drink for all the rest' and the vault is a sort of shrine to Liverpool Football Club with much football memorabilia. In good weather you may sit at the tables and benches outside. Food is served at lunchtimes.

SOUTHPORT
Bold Arms

59 Botanic Road, Churchtown

Centre of Churchtown, just off A5267

Own car park at rear

Tetley Mild, Dark Mild, Bitter; Jennings Bitter; Ind Coope Burton Ale (plus Walkers Winter Warmer in season)

Churchtown is a picturesque little village which existed before Southport was thought of. The Bolds and the Heskeths were the two land owning families and the **Bold Arms** and **Heskeths Arms** are on opposite sides of the crossroads in the centre of the village. The **Bold Arms** is a long low and rambling old coaching inn. The building itself, the stable block at the rear, the cobbled forecourt and even the wooden railing at the front are all listed structures.

The interior comprises four or five separate but linked rooms with lots of alcoves and nooks and crannies. Some bits look quite old but the pub has been gradually updated and improved over the years so it is now quite a mixture of styles. The large bow fronted floor to ceiling windows at the rear are an attractive feature. Coloured glass panels in the windows feature different elements of the Bold livery.

There is a friendly relaxed atmosphere and it is such a large building with so much space it can cater for all comers. It is popular with the local CAMRA branch and there are CAMRA charity quiz nights. There are also pop music quizzes and fun quizzes on Mondays. Many people come to eat at lunchtimes. There is a regular menu with a wide range of typical pub food plus daily blackboard specials, vegetarian options and childrens meals. Main meals are £2 to £3, childrens meals £1.35. In good weather you can sit out on the forecourt.

SOUTHPORT

Ship Inn

Cable Street

Off Neville Street, off Lord Street. Very near to the war memorial and the BR station

Parking nearby is difficult

Bass Mild, Bitter and Draught Bass

Just around the corner from the prosperity and showiness of Lord Street there is a wonderful little seaside pub which is completely unpretentious and as homely and welcoming as you could wish for. It has a traditional three room layout with a proper vault, a very pleasant parlour and a large back room with television and darts. Before Bass acquired it, the pub belonged to the **Walkdens**

brewery of Birkdale and the original **Walkdens** cut glass bay window is still in place. It is difficult to imagine a more pleasant pub experience than to sit in the bay window seat in the front parlour of the Ship, supping Draught Bass to accompany a satisfying home made meal and without any interference from fruit machines or a juke box.

The pub is well appreciated by locals and visitors alike and one of the main attractions is the food. There is no cash and carry or supermarket convenience food here. It is all no-frills, real, home cooked food, lovingly prepared and reasonably priced. There is always a home made soup kept heated on the corner of the bar, hot and cold filled rolls and toasted sandwiches, bacon and cheese pie and meat and potato pots. A popular item is the mixed grill on toast (sausage, liver, mushroom, black pudding and tomato). Food is available both lunchtime and evening. Children are welcome during the day and early evening. The **Ship** has been run by the same licensee for 29 years and that wealth of experience is very apparent to all who visit the pub.

UPHOLLAND

Old Dog

Alma Hill

Upholland is just north of the M58 between Orrell and Skelmersdale and Alma Hill comes out at the central crossroads on the A577 through the village

Parking on nearby side street (Alma Court)

Greenalls Mild, Bitter

Closed lunchtimes on weekdays

This charming little pub owes its present character to the fact that it has been in the stewardship of one family for 60 years (the present licensee was born in the pub) and also because it is a listed building and is therefore relatively safe from excessive modernisation. It is well maintained and comfortable and it has that welcoming hospitable quality that you associate with a well established, family-run pub.

The pub was originally three cottages. it dates from 1742 and was once known as the **Talbot** which is a type of large hunting dog, now extinct. It seems as though, at some time, the pub has officially adopted its nick name. Greenalls acquired the pub from the Cunningham Brewery of Warrington in the 1950s.

The **Old Dog** operates as a community pub but it also attracts customers from a distance who appreciate its warmth and conviviality. There are four rooms, all with different characteristics: the tiny 'horse box' adjacent to the bar; the tap room for games and television; the back parlour with its wonderful collection of brass, obviously lovingly collected over the years and 'number 3 room', an extra area created from the former living quarters. There is also a function room upstairs which caters for local weddings and birthdays. There is no juke box, no gambling machines and, because it is not open at lunchtimes, no food. Children are allowed for the early part of the evening. The pub is up for sale because it does not fit into Greenalls corporate mould. Hopefully this will safeguard the pub for the future, especially if the present licensee continues to have a stake in the pub.

WALTON
Prince Arthur

93 Rice Lane

A59 north of Walton town centre, adjacent to hospital

Parking available in streets opposite

Walker Mild, Bitter

The pub looks interesting from outside and the interior certainly lives up to expectations. It is a veritable peoples palace. A profusion of red tiles embellished with gold and blue together with the extravagant use of stained glass and mahogany and mosaic give this pub a distinction you would not expect in this location. It is not a brewery tap; it is not in the city centre; all this ornate decor is for the benefit of Walton locals.

There is a central, triangular shaped bar with a corridor around and two sides of this comprise the public bar, the most unspartan you will ever see, broken up by glazed screens. A smoke room opens up off the third side of the bar. This has been fitted out with new soft furnishings, lighting and ceiling fans in a way which complements the rest of the pub. There was a major refurbishment in 1983 and it was so successful in cherishing and restoring the original features and blending in new materials that it won a special CAMRA Pub Preservation Award. But it also functions well as a good local serving good cheap locally brewed beer. Even the presence of a juke box and three fruit machines does not detract from the experience of drinking there. For food, filled rolls are usually available.

WARRINGTON

Bulls Head

33 Church Street

On A57, close to roundabout junction with Mersey Street

2 to 3 minutes walk away from any parking facilities

Greenalls Mild and Bitter

Here is a 17th century inn which provides links with the past and at the same time functions as a vital part of today's local community. The sporting and social activities encompass bowling, darts, dominoes, pool, a quiz league and karaoke on Saturday nights. It is basically a plain, homely pub with low ceilings, low doorways, quarry tile floors and over the years it has been gradually extended and adapted to changing times with various bits added and renewed and remodelled. The result is a pleasing jumble of rooms and nooks and crannies with fixtures and finishes reflecting past

ages. The process is still going on and recently it has lost a cosy corner of the front lounge and a nice little front parlour because of the present vogue for getting rid of constricting passageways and maximising the use of space.

However, the pub still has five rooms plus a functions room. At the rear to the left is the 'ladies room', at one time a refuge for the ladies but now used mainly as a committee room because the pub is the headquarters of the local darts and domino league. To the right is the holy of holies, the smoke room, also known as the 'bowling room' because this is the sanctum of the bowling club, its walls covered with trophies and fading photographs of bowling teams dating back to 1908. Off the front lounge there is a darts room and a pool room. The function room is housed in a separate building in the back yard and beyond is the bowling green, an unexpected oasis of green, hemmed in by industrial buildings and the mainstay of the pub for as long as anyone can remember. In summer months it makes a pleasant spot for families.

WARRINGTON
Ring o' Bells

Church Street

A57, opposite Sainsburys, next to parish church

Limited forecourt parking

Greenalls Mild, Original; Stones Bitter

The **Ring o' Bells** is an ancient pub with a cobbled forecourt, set back from the main road among the parish church outbuildings in a little corner of old Warrington. Over the years it has gradually expanded into neighbouring buildings and a few years ago it was comprehensively refurbished by the brewery. The result has been quite successful, retaining some character and genuine antiquity together with a comfortable and relaxing atmosphere.

The lounge area is shaped like a piece of jigsaw puzzle with four separate but interconnecting areas. A narrow passageway takes you around the bar into a larger room with a separate entrance. Upstairs there is a club room. Many of the walls are wood panelled and there are some genuine timber beams and lintels. In wintertime there are three roaring fires, real coal fires. The stamp of the interior designer is in evidence but it is generally in keeping with the antiquity of the place. There are juke boxes and fruit machines but they are unobtrusive and the noise level is kept down. In summer an added bonus is to sit out in the beer garden at the rear among mature birch trees and in the shadow of the church steeple. Lunchtime food is served Monday to Friday and children are welcome.

WAVERTREE
Royal Hotel

213 Smithdown Road

A562, opposite Toxteth Cemetery

Street parking nearby

Tetley Mild, Bitter

This is an impressive Victorian corner pub with a sumptuous ceramic tile and mosaic facade to first floor level in blues, golds and reds. The interior has been well treated by the brewery. A recent refurbishment has enhanced all the best features and matched original fittings where possible.

There is a door on each street and a corner door into the public bar. The main entrance brings you into a central corridor with hatches to serve the parlour/newsroom and smoke room off. The public bar has a long marble topped counter and a television and is the busiest area. The front parlour has some attractive little cubby holes and alcoves screened off within. The rear smoke room is lined with the ubiquitous book-shelves beloved of brewery designers but at least the books have been read and not bought by the yard. All the woodwork has been re-grained, there are two open fires and a juke box. The **Royal** is a community pub serving the residential area all around, but visitors would not feel out of place.

WESTHOUGHTON

White Lion Hotel

2 Market Street

A58, corner of Bolton Road, town centre

Car park at rear of pub

Holt Mild, Bitter

The **White Lion** is a distinctive pub even within the Holt estate. It is an unpretentious, four square building occupying the site of an old inn. The interior probably dates from around the turn of the century. The carved and shuttered island bar with its etched glass panels is the most noticeable feature but the character of the pub also derives from its intimate layout of five areas: bar parlour, smoke room, back parlour, vault with a separate entrance and a standing up area in front of the bar. Some of the original bench seating and most of the internal doors are in place.

It has a fairly plain decor with the walls and low ceilings painted a uniform stippled cream and minimal embellishment in the form of pictures and bric-a-brac but the different rooms do have some individuality, each attracting their own regular customers. A couple of fireplaces have been blocked up but other than that the only noticeable changes are the occasional lick of paint and reupholstery. There is a television in the vault and piped music in other areas but it is usually possible to find one quiet room. At lunchtime filled rolls are available.

WIGAN

Springfield Hotel

47 Springfield Road

West of town centre, off B5375, close to Wigan Athletic Football Ground

Own car park

Walker Mild, Best Bitter, Winter Warmer (in season)

You do not expect to find an imposing old pub like this in such an ordinary suburban street. It was a flagship for the former Oldfield brewery when it was built in 1903. It was acquired by Walkers in 1926 and has been well looked after since then. The fact that it is a listed building probably encourages the brewery to do the right thing.

There have been some changes: the bowling green has become a car park; the original billiard room has become a sumptuous concert room with its own bar; the smoke room is now a lounge; the commercial room is still a relatively quiet haven and the bar is still the bar. The interior designers have recently been in and put a 1990s gloss on the place with fancy wallpaper, reproduction fireplaces, vast swathes of modern carpet and anonymous archive family photographs in reproduction frames, but they have restored the bar where it had been damaged and they have left intact all the main ostentatious features of the interior. The pub does not serve food.

WIGAN

Swan and Railway Hotel

80 Wallgate

Town centre, opposite North Western Rail Station. Not far from Wigan Pier

Parking on BR Station forecourt

Bass Mild, Draught Bass; Banks's Mild, Bitter; John Smith's Bitter; Stones Bitter

The pub was closed and de-licensed by Tetley Walker in 1982 and soon after much of the interior was destroyed by a fire. Its potential was realised by a private individual and it was rescued and renovated to a high standard. The mosaic floor and the tiled panels in the main corridor escaped the fire and there is some original woodwork but much else has been renewed and every effort has been made to restore a genuine Edwardian feel to the place. The public bar has been retained with its separate entrance and it is often the busiest part of the pub. In addition there is a front parlour, lots of corridor drinking space and a large back room broken up into the three spaces and used as a dining area during the day.

The four metre high ceilings give the pub a feeling of spaciousness but the space is divided well so that it does not feel empty during quiet periods. There are not many quiet periods. The **Swan and Railway** offers a good range of reasonably priced beers and meals; it is situated between Wigan's two railway stations on the edge of the shopping area and it is a well run, pleasant place to be so it has regulars and also attracts a good mix of office workers, travellers and shoppers. The set menu includes soups, salads, sandwiches, pies and standard but good quality pub grub with chips. The price for a main dish is £2 to £3. There is also a basic wine list and tea and coffee are available. There is a television in the vault and elsewhere a juke box and three fruit machines but in a pub of this size its always possible to find a quiet corner. If you are staying in Wigan you could do worse than stay here. To book accommodation telephone Wigan (0942) 495032.

SOME FURTHER SUGGESTIONS

Abbey, Walker
153 Walton Lane, Kirkdale, Liverpool (A580, opposite Stanley Park)

Beehive, Walker
7 Paradise Street, Liverpool City Centre (pedestrianised area near bus station)

Boars Head, Walker
2 Market Place, Leigh (town centre)

Bucks Head, Walker
256 Warrington Road, Abram, Wigan (south of Wigan, A573)

Colliers Arms, Greenalls
Pimbo Road, Kings Moss, Billinge (between Rainford, Billinge and Skelmersdale, OS reference SD 507011)

Commercial Hotel, Higsons/Cains/Theakston
Station Road, Rainhill (south of St Helens, pub is just off A57, next to railway station)

Crows Nest, Higsons/Cains/Boddingtons
61 Victoria Road, Crosby (between Blundellsands Station and B5193, Little Crosby Road)

Dart, Walker
39 Lodge Lane, Toxteth, Liverpool (south east of city centre, B5173)

Globe, Higsons/Cains
17 Cases Street, Liverpool City Centre (of Ranelagh Street, opposite Central Station)

Guest House, Higsons/Cains
Union Street, Southport (off Lord Street)

Halton Castle, Higsons/Cains
86 Mill Lane, West Derby, Liverpool (between A5058 and Croxteth Park)

Holt's Arms, Burtonwood
Crank Road, Billinge (just off B5206, between Billinge and Orrell)

Lister Hotel, Walker
28 Prescot Road, Kensington, Liverpool (A57, two miles east of city centre)

Lower Angel, Walker
27 Butterworth Street, Warrington (town centre)

Masonic Arms, Tetley
19 Lodge Lane, Toxteth, Liverpool (south east of city centre, B5173)

Melrose Abbey, Tetley
331 Westminster Road, Kirkdale, Liverpool (just west of A59)

Mosley Arms, Tetley
156 Mill Street, Toxteth, Liverpool (south of city centre, off A561)

Old Springs, Burtonwood
Spring Road, Kitt Green, Wigan (west of Wigan, one mile north of A577, adjacent to Heinz factory, OS reference SD 547062)

Pig and Whistle, Tetley
Covent Garden, Liverpool City Centre (off Water Street, northern fringe of city centre)

Poste House, Higsons/Cains
23 Cumberland Street, Liverpool City Centre (between Dale Street and Victoria Street)

Railway, Higsons
111 Merton Road, Bootle (A5057, close to railway and Leeds/Liverpool canal)

Railway, Burtonwood
2 Station Road, Parbold (north west of Wigan, just off A5209)

Running Horses, Walker/Ind Coope
25 Bells Lane, Lydiate (8 miles north of Liverpool, off A569, just north of junction with B5407)

Sefton Arms, Tetley
106 Westminster Road, Kirkdale, Liverpool (just west of A59)

Silverwell, Walker/Ind Coope Burton Ale
Darlington Street East, Wigan (southern fringe of town centre)

Town Green Inn, Tetley (not real ale)
17 Town Green Lane, Aughton (town centre, south of Ormskirk, just off A59)

Upsteps, Matthew Brown/Theakston
20 Upper Aughton Road, Birkdale (off A565)

Victoria, Tetley (plus guest beers)
20 Ann Street West, Widnes (south eastern fringe of town centre, near B and Q)

Waldeck, Walker
113 Lawrence Road, Wavertree, Liverpool (parallel to and north of A562, south east of city centre)

Wheatsheaf, Greenalls/Stones
Mill Lane, Sutton, St. Helens (south of St Helens, B5204, west of St Helens Junction Station)

Willowbank, Walker/Ind Coope Burton Ale
329 Southdown Road, Wavertree, Liverpool (A562, south east of city centre, opposite Sefton General Hospital.

When exploring Liverpool city centre pubs there are four additional ones worth taking in: **Beehive, Globe, Pig and Whistle** and the **Poste House**. The **Beehive** has a long, narrow, high-ceilinged interior with a dining area at the rear. It is a popular eating place at lunchtimes. In the early years of the century it was a 'Walkers Grill' and at one time in its history it is believed to have been a Chinese theatre. It has Victorian style decor and good use is made of Walkers mirrors.

The Globe is a very popular pub, often crowded with its many regulars. There is a tiny snug at the back which is usually quieter than the main bar. It was refurbished in 1988 and gained carpets, fancy light fittings and screens providing a bit of privacy but the idiosyncratic sloping floor was left in place. It is the place to go if you want a friendly, noisy, lively atmosphere.

Many Liverpool pubs have connections with seafarers but not many go back as far as the **Pig and Whistle**. It is a very ancient pub, originally a chop house, probably pre-dating the present building. It has an interesting layout of downstairs bar, small parlour off the half landing and a further room upstairs with its own bar. It has recently been refurbished to a very high standard retaining the nautical links with maps and photographs of merchant ships and Liverpool Docks mounted on the walls. The licensee is not very committed to real ale and you may find that only keg beers are available.

The **Poste House** is another very old Liverpool pub. At one time it was reputed to be the haunt of smugglers. In the last century it was known as the 'New Post Office Restaurant'. These days It is a cosy haven with two small rooms on two floors, each with its own bar. It has recently been completely refurbished with modern reproduction materials but it works well.

For those game to seek out some traditional pubs in Liverpool's inner city areas there are quite a few examples of showy but seedy pubs which have obviously had a glorious past but have recently been left to gently deteriorate. The most magnificent is the **Lister**.

It has the same window glass as the **Vines** and many other extravagant gin palace features including a mahogany panelled smoke room. It is rather tatty and run down and noisy but still functioning well as a pub and capable of being restored.

In Toxteth, just a few yards from each other, the **Masonic** is an ex-Walkers pub, shabby but rich in 1920s period detail and completely unspoilt and the **Dart** has an original public bar and back parlour but the lounge has been refurbished at some time. Both pubs these days are good community boozers. Also in Toxteth and also an ex-Walkers house is the **Mosley Arms** with many ornate original features.

In Kirkdale area, the **Abbey** is an imposing pub which has been recently recarpeted and reupholstered but it retains some good original features and the **Melrose Abbey** is a traditional three-roomed, unchanging pub on a busy road corner, popular with darts fans and off duty railmen. The **Sefton Arms** is now owned by Belhaven Inns, a Scottish pub company but, as is usual with these pubs, only serves Tetley beers. It has an impressive concert room with a small stage and dance floor and a lofty vaulted ceiling. There is also a traditional vault, smoke room and a function room upstairs and much oak, etched glass and original fireplaces and bar fittings.

In Bootle, dozens of pubs have closed and the **Railway** has been for sale for some time and may not last out much longer before it too is closed. This would be a pity because it has a solid 1920s interior in good condition. There is a public bar and a smoke room divided by partitions and with an impressive oak fireplace.

Although many Higsons pubs have been extensively modernised and transformed out of recognition, there are a handful still recognisable as traditional pubs. The **Commercial** is a good looking, lively community local, slightly opened out but still with a smoke room, parlour and separate public bar. It was built in the inter-war years for the Joseph Jones Knotty Ash Brewery and still has windows engraved with the name. On the walls there is an extensive collection of local archive photographs.

In Crosby the **Crows Nest** is a good suburban local with a well preserved tiled exterior and a very pleasing ornate bar in the front snug. The lounge at the back is indistinguishable from many others but the two small front rooms, public bar and snug are full of character. There is a collection of photographs of other 'Crows Nest' pubs and bars all over the world. The **Halton Castle** in West Derby is similar in some ways with a central bar at the front

serving two rooms and there are two further rooms at the rear. Equal space is given to both Liverpool and Everton football club memorabilia on the walls.

If you are in the vicinity of the **Royal Hotel** q.v. in Wavertree there are two Walker pubs nearby which are worth a visit. The **Willowbank**, set back off the road, is reputed to be 250 years old. Most of the pub has been unaltered for decades. There are four separate rooms all of different character. Close by is the **Waldeck**, which retains some fine leaded, stained glass windows and the public bar features a mural of the Liverpool Dock scene.

Other notable Walker pubs in the South Lancashire area are the **Running Horses** in Lydiate, a good, traditional, canal-side pub on the edge of the countryside, catering for everyone and with a good range of facilities and outside drinking areas; the **Silverwell** in Wigan, a large, multi-roomed, town centre pub well endowed with wood panelling and decorative glass throughout; the **Lower Angel** in Warrington, a small, busy, two-roomed pub and a Good Beer Guide perennial; the **Boars Head** in Leigh which is a grand example of Edwardian architecture, a listed building which won a

CAMRA 'Pub of the Year' award in 1983 and the **Bucks Head** in Abram, a large well run village pub with a well used bowling green. Families are well catered for here.

Greenalls have carried out a major 'improvement' programme to their pubs in recent years generally eradicating character and individuality but there are a handful which are still interesting or unusual in some way. The **Colliers Arms** at Kings Moss has retained its rustic simplicity and separate drinking areas. It is in a very pleasant rural location and it lays on good, home cooked, reasonably priced meals. The **Wheatsheaf** at St Helens is a friendly, inter-war community pub whose social life revolves around the bowling green. It does not look as though it has been altered but in fact it is held together with ties and braces because it has been gradually sinking below the road level for years due to mining subsidence. The floors slope in all directions.

A Burtonwood pub which stands out from the others is the **Old Springs** near Wigan which is a cosy, unspoilt, early 19th century stone pub with a walled bowling green. The pub is named after the ancient wells of the area, one of which lies behind the pub. Home cooked cheap meals are available and a three course Sunday lunch costs £5. Another good Burtonwood pub is the **Railway** at Parbold. It is a cosy village pub with many different rooms and drinking areas all full of railway 'numerasignia' — photographs, maps and signs. It is close to the Leeds-Liverpool Canal.

The **Holt's Arms** at Billinge is a wonderful Burtonwood pub but its future is in doubt because it has been taken over by a pub retailing group who have plans to build a large car park and no doubt transform it into an upmarket restaurant pub. Parts of the building date from the 15th century. It has a genuine, uncontrived country pub ambience. There is a bowling green and acres of attached land, mainly in the Green Belt. It is a shame to see a pub like this just marking time. It has not been adequately maintained for years and the uncertainty about its future is having a blighting effect. It would be wise to visit soon because it may become irretrievably altered.

In Southport, in the vicinity of the **Ship** q.v., the **Guest House** is a traditional town centre ale house. Although the interior is not as interesting as the outside it is still a good, solid, popular pub with three rooms, one of them with wood panelling.

Also near Southport, **Upsteps** is a horse-racing pub, close to Red Rum's stables. There are 9 steps up to the front door. Although much remodelled (see photograph of original pub mounted on the wall) the pub still has a good traditional feel to it. There is a television in the public bar and a further one in the body of the pub, both invariably tuned to the racing.

In addition to the **Dog and Gun** q.v., in Aughton, there is another interesting pub, the **Town Green Inn**. This is a characterful, solid, stone building, very comfortable and smart with log fires in winter, a traditional vault and a large lounge cleverly divided into separate spaces. The only problem is that it serves keg beer.

There is no problem with the beer at the **Victoria** in Widnes. In addition to the Tetley beers there are regular guest beers. It is a busy community pub with a range of pub games, a sea angling club, country music on Wednesdays and 60s music at the weekends. The public bar is the heart of the pub but the large lounge with a stage can also get crowded.

Ribble, Calder, Pendle

BACUP

New Inn

11 Rochdale Road

Town centre

Parking not difficult

Thwaites Best Mild, Bitter

Those who knew the original pub may disagree, but Thwaites appear to have carried out a sensitive refurbishment here, retaining the original layout and the best traditional features and at the same time making the place clean and comfortable. From the

outside it looks like an ordinary stone built terraced pub but the interior is quite spacious with a small bar serving four rooms, two of them away from the bar. Many layers of paint, going back over decades, have been stripped from the woodwork which has then been regrained and the unusual strip panel ceilings have been restored. In the small corner snug next to the bar some fading murals, dating from when the pub was built in 1880, have been retained.

The floors are generally carpeted except the front games room/public bar where the musicians gather for weekly Saturday lunch time folk sessions. The only discordant note comes from the loud juke box music which is relayed throughout the pub. A good time to visit Bacup, and the **New Inn**, is on Easter Saturday when the Coconutters do their annual tour of the town. It is a local ceremony of ancient origin involving local men dressed up and with blackened faces, clapping with wooden discs, originally coconut shells. They are followed by a good natured crowd of people, thronging through the town and calling in each pub collecting for charities. The **New Inn** becomes quite crowded on that day. Children are allowed in the rooms away from the bar. Filled rolls are usually available.

BELMONT

Black Dog

2 Church Street

Belmont is five miles north of Bolton on the A675 road to Preston. The pub is on a corner of the main road

Parking on Church Street

Holt Mild, Bitter

The **Black Dog** is a popular moorland village pub well known for its characterful landlord and because it is an outpost of the Joseph Holt brewery. Its origin was as a farmhouse pub and, like so many early public houses, it was the only public building apart from the church so it was used as the local courthouse at one time. Just ignore the ugly modern flat roofed extension lounge and enjoy the two traditional areas in front of the bar, the small pool room and

the tiny snug at the back, all crammed with bric-a-brac on the walls and festooned from the beams.

What marks the pub out from others is classical music — occasionally in the form of a small live orchestra, otherwise on tape or simply whistled expertly by your host. Obviously this is a juke-box free pub. The music is just one element of the hospitality though. You can eat very well at reasonable prices lunchtimes and early evening (try the homemade soup); there are tables outside in the good weather; children are welcome and, if you cannot tear yourself away you can stay the night in visitor accommodation in converted stables. Not surprisingly, the pub keeps very busy most times of year. People visit from near and far and include locals, ramblers, hang gliders, pot-holers and ordinary folk out for a meal.

BRIERFIELD

Waggon and Horses

Colne Road

A56, just south of Junction 12, M65

Car park adjacent to pub

Thwaites Best Mild, Bitter, Craftsmans

Thwaites are quite proud of the **Waggon and Horses**. The pub won a CAMRA award in 1983 for careful renovation work which respected the pub's character and retained all the best features of the interior. 'Best Renovated Pub Award' is permanently displayed outside for all to see. It is more usual to find pubs like this in the heart of an urban area rather than this rather isolated roadside location.

The **Waggon** acquired its impressive interior when it belonged to Massey's Brewery of Burnley. It was subsequently owned by Bass before passing on to Thwaites. The best features of the pub are the individuality of each room and the high quality 19th century tiling, glass, joinery and marble fireplaces. There is a lobby area around the bar, a 'library' with a real coal fire in winter, a games room, a parlour which leads to a beer garden and a tiny snug with gas mantle lighting. The pub is popular for its lunchtime food which comprises baked potatoes, chillies, gammon, chicken Kiev and steaks with main meals costing around £3. There are a wide variety of customers, young and old. There is a piano, piped music and a fruit machine but some parts of the pub are quiet.

BURNLEY

Swan Inn

44 St James' Street

Town centre, on the main pedestrianised shopping street

Car parks nearby

Thwaites Mild, Bitter (keg beer)

The **Swan** has a very advantageous position on the high street. It is an obviously old, stone building, cleaned up but with faded livery and advertisements still in place. A few years ago Thwaites carried out an extensive refit of the pub and it turned out quite well. It is an old inn which used to play an important part in the life of the town. The Town Committee, who were responsible for policing, would

meet here and the toilets at the rear were at one time barred cells, reputed to be the local lockup.

During the day the **Swan** serves good, cheap no-frills food and caters for shoppers and business people. It also has a pool table, television, three electronic machines and a juke box and some-times these noisy amusements tend to dominate. The building originally had a warren of small rooms. There is now a fairly large stone flagged lobby area with a bar and opening off here, a tap room, pool room, back parlour, a delightful, narrow little snug and a conservatory with a wood block floor. In summer there is also a sitting out area at the back of the building.

Many layers of old paint have been stripped off the wood panelled walls and ceilings and doors and all the original simple, cast iron fireplaces have been retained with open fires. The furniture is good solid, old fashioned tables, chairs and settles. The food menu offers a wide choice of sandwiches, snacks, salads and main meals including vegetarian options and a children's menu – also sweets, tea and coffee. The main meals range from £1.60 to £3. The **Swan** is an interesting pub with lots of potential but it is a pity they do not throw out some of the noisy activities and introduce cask conditioned beer.

CLITHEROE

New Inn

Parsons Lane

Near the market and within a shadow of Clitheroe Castle

Parking on forecourt and market car parks nearby

Boddingtons Mild, Bitter; Hartleys XB; Moorhouse's Premier

Closed winter weekday afternoons and Wednesday afternoons in summer

On Clitheroe High Street there are some eminent inns and coaching houses but, as is so often the case in primary commercial locations, they have lost their heart and soul. The **New Inn** is just around the corner from most of the bustle and activity

and, perhaps because of this, it remains an archetypal market town pub, homely and welcoming and catering for all comers.

It is a large, late 18th century, listed stone building set back from the road. There is a central lobby area, adjacent to the staircase, where the bar is situated and the four public rooms are all away from the bar. The decor and the furnishings are plain and comfortable with much roughly grained woodwork. The two front rooms act as lounges with roaring real coal fires in winter. There is a pool room opposite the bar and a large dining room at the rear of the pub although they do not stand on ceremony and you can eat wherever you prefer.

A wide range of home cooked meals and snacks are available on the set menu and also daily specials, at around £3 for an enormous plateful of food. There is also a childrens menu and children are welcome in the dining room. There is no juke box, simply a radio, tuned to a local station, at the bar. The best time to visit this pub is probably on a market day, Tuesdays and Saturdays, when it is thronging with regulars and visitors and you can savour to the full the character and individuality of the place.

FOULRIDGE
Hole in the Wall

Town Gate

B6251, just west of A56

Street parking available

__Bass Mild, Bitter__

The **Hole in the Wall** is a prominent Victorian corner pub off the main road in the heart of Foulridge, close to the village green. It is in a good position to take advantage of the Leeds-Liverpool Canal-borne trade from Foulridge Wharf nearby. There is the usual smoke room, bar parlour and 'general room' and the pub retains

most of its architectural features such as etched glass, attractive wall tiling (although some has been painted over) and high ceilings. Near the entrance is what remains of an off sales department. Children are allowed in the bar parlour. Pool is played to the accompaniment of loud music in the general room but the remainder of the pub is quiet. There are real coal fires in wintertime.

In 1912, a cow called Buttercup became a local celebrity after falling into the canal and swimming the length of the mile long Foulridge tunnel. She was revived at the pub with a tot of whiskey.

GOOSNARGH

Grapes Inn

Centre of the village

Between Preston and Longridge, just north of B5269

parking available on forecourt and nearby roadside

Boddingtons Bitter

The pub occupies a central place and a central part of the village life. It is adjacent to the village church and Georgian manor house and has obviously evolved over the centuries from simple origins to its present status as pre-eminent village local and welcoming hostelry for visitors. It manages to combine both functions well. There is a pleasant back room with a lived-in look, a games room, a large lounge which is given over to dining and one of those tiny private snugs behind the bar.

There is a food servery in the lounge which dispenses the comprehensive regular menu and the daily blackboard specials. The price of main meals is around £3.50. Meals are available lunchtimes and evening. The bowling green at the rear of the pub provides a good diversion on summer evenings and you can also sit out at benches and tables on the front forecourt. Children are welcome in rooms away from the bar.

Like many other old pubs this one has had a few previous names. originally the **Saracens Head**, it was renamed the **General Elliot** in honour of one of Cromwell's commanders after it was used as a base by Cromwell in 1648.

GREAT HARWOOD
Victoria

St John Street

Southern part of the town just east of the A6064, OS reference SD 733318

Street parking adjacent

Matthew Brown Mild, Bitter

The **Victoria** is a splendid turn-of-the-century railway pub. The railway is long gone and a pub of this size seems a bit isolated and incongruent in what is now a backwater of the town but its isolation has probably helped to preserve its wonderful architectural qualities intact. After years of gentle deterioration it was recently

renovated in a very sympathetic manner which managed to accommodate the full range of facilities necessary for a pub of today, at the same time enhancing all the original features.

There are five rooms including parlour, bar parlour, smoke room and 'public kitchen' and the most striking thing is the sheer variety of finishes from room to room such as the impressive full height wall tiling in the entrance lobby to the tiled floors, wood panelled ceilings and slatted wooden seats. The pub caters for all tastes with a pool table, fruit machines, a floodlit bowling green (where you can sit out in summer), monthly ceilidh nights, and summer bar-b-ques. Children are welcomed and well catered for and a selection of good, reasonably priced meals are available at lunch times.

LONGRIDGE

Towneley Arms

41 Berry Lane

Town centre, off B5269

Parking on forecourt and side streets

Tetley Mild, Bitter

The **Towneley Arms** is a good, solid, Lancashire town, locals pub. It is an old stone building in the heart of town near to the site of the former railway station. It is firmly integrated into the local community being a meeting place for the local Lions Club and host to a wide range of customers from the town and the surrounding farmland. The Town Council Chambers, adjoining the back of the building, is the venue for the Longridge Homing Society.

The bar faces the rear of the building and serves three rear rooms and two front rooms. The rear rooms are very atmospheric and restful with dark wood panelling, comfortable settees, traditional furniture and roaring fires in winter. The area around the bar has been opened up a little but this has not changed the character of the pub. There is no food and no juke box but the local radio station is often relayed from the bar.

The name of course is derived from the famous old Lancashire Catholic family based in Burnley but with extensive estates in Lancashire.

TOCKHOLES

Royal Arms

One mile south of village of Tockholes, OS reference SD 665215

Due west of Darwen but approached off A6062, north of Darwen or off A675, north of Belmont

West Pennine Moors public car park adjacent to pub

Thwaites, Best Mild, Bitter

At the edge of the West Pennine Moors and miles from anywhere, it is a pleasant surprise to come across a nice unspoilt pub like this one. There are walks to nearby Darwen Hill and Tower and the Roddlesworth Woodland Nature Trail runs close by. There are not

many locals around here so the pub relies on car-borne visitors and, especially at weekends, it is very popular with families throughout the year.

Inside there are some unusual features including much dressed stonework in door openings and massive log burning fireplaces and dark brown panel-effect walls. The four interconnecting rooms, dominated by two central chimney breasts are cosy and welcoming, each with a fireplace and furnished with pews and other traditional furniture. There is also a small beer garden. Good value home cooked food is available at most times except Tuesdays — soups, snacks and full meals ranging in price from £1 to around £3.50. It is a very hospitable pub which tries to cater for all users ranging from small children to walkers with muddy boots. For cold, wet hikers, hot chocolate, coffee or tea is available. There is no juke box or fruit machines.

Thwaites have owned the pub since 1873. The pub took its name from the Royal Mill which used to stand where the car park is now sited.

WADDINGTON

The Buck Inn

Church Street

Not to be confused with the **'Higher Buck'** in the village square, the **Buck** is known locally as the **'Lower Buck'**. It is in the centre of the village, just west of the main road and north of the parish church. Waddington is $1^1/_2$ miles north of Clitheroe on the B6478

Limited parking adjacent to pub

Robinson's Best Bitter; Taylor Best Bitter; Tetley Bitter plus guest beers (beer range may vary)

The **Lower Buck** is actually just outside the Lancashire border but is too good to miss. It is in the same league as the **Ship**, Overton, another contender for the title of 'perfect pub'. The interior has survived in its original Victorian form because it is managed by a trust involving the local landed gentry, the Parker family, and the

landlord can hardly change a lightbulb without first gaining permission from the trustees. Some years ago an errant landlord got away with a slight alteration to the bar fittings but it is otherwise unaltered.

You are drinking in classic Victorian coach house surroundings and with a bit of imagination you can transport yourself back to a previous age. The building dates from 1760 and it still retains its original coach house and stables, also little changed, and a cobbled forecourt. The three downstairs rooms all have their own character. The main front room has more links with the past: attractive glasswork in the bar, polished brick fire surround with a real coal fire and a carved wooden sideboard built into the wall. The back room is a simple but comfortable tap room and the other front room, also with a fine old fireplace, is an overspill area and family room. A recent innovation has been the conversion of an upstairs room to a small restaurant.

The current licensee and the trustees have demonstrated that it is perfectly possible for a pub to thrive and offer a comprehensive range of facilities for a wide cross section of customers without destroying our heritage or compromising the essential historic character of a building. The **Buck** offers good food at all times, accommodation, access for the disabled, space for families (until 8pm) and a good range of beers as well. Some breweries manage to spend a small fortune trying unsuccessfully to emulate this sort of operation. There are no juke boxes or fruit machines but there is a well used piano in the front room used for sing songs on Friday and Saturday evenings. Food in the restaurant is a-la-carte and downstairs it is excellent, home cooked fare. The portions are generous and very good value for money. Traditional, three course roast beef lunch is served each Sunday. The Good Beer Guide incorrectly describes the pub as a listed building but perhaps it should be.

WORSTHORNE
Crooked Billet

Smith Street

Worsthorne is two miles east of Burnley. The pub is in the centre of the village

Forecourt parking or street parking by the church

Tetley Mild, Bitter; Boddingtons Bitter

It is fitting that a conservation conscious village such as Worsthorne should have a pub like the **Crooked Billet**, for it is absolutely unspoilt both externally and internally and is run as a proper community village local. it was built in 1911, replacing a pub that had grown out of a group of back-to-back cottages but it still has the remainder of the row of cottages as neighbours. It was originally a pub of the local Grimshaw brewery which was taken over by Massey's Burnley Brewery which then became a part of Bass. However, it then went over to Tetley Walker in a pub swop deal during the 1970s. The etched Grimshaw windows are still in place.

The interior is a delight because it is virtually unchanged since 1911. There is a central shuttered bar with cut glass panels and with a tiny, cosy vault on one side and an oak panelled lounge on the other side. Two rooms are away from the bar. An original parlour has had its doorway widened slightly and is now a dining room and the remaining room looks as though it has been in a time warp since 1911 with its decorative fireplace, settle back seating and traditional domino tables. This room is mainly for the use of the long-standing local Don and Domino League every Tuesday evening (Don is a local card game). The rooms by the way are not given names but are numbered and the numbers are etched into the door glass.

The name of the pub is unusual in Lancashire but is more common in the south of England. There has been much written about it because there are many possible explanations for its origin. It could mean a crooked walking stick, shepherds crook or a serfs weapon. It is often signified by a rough hewn stick hanging over a doorway.

Lunchtime food consists of soup, sandwiches, meals around £3 such as lasagne, steak and kidney pie or curry, and sweets and coffee are also available. The pub is cosy in wintertime with real fires burning in its three fireplaces and in summer the south-facing forecourt provides an excellent sunny sitting out area with tables and benches provided. There are no juke boxes or gaming machines. Children are allowed into the dining room.

SOME FURTHER SUGGESTIONS

Admiral Lord Rodney, Theakston
Mill Green, Waterside, Colne (southern edge of Colne, next to Colne Water)

Cross Gaits Inn, Burtonwood
Beverley Road, Blacko (OS reference SD 866414, half mile east of A682 just north of Barrowford and Nelson)

Foresters Arms, Wilson's/Webster's/Theakston
Pleasant Street, Haslingden (off Deardengate - near town centre crossroads – off A680, off A56)

Golden Cup, Thwaites
610 Blackburn Road, Darwen (A666, northern edge of town - M65 extension to pass very close by)

Great Eastern, Thwaites
Arnold Street, Accrington (off Burnley Road, A679 near junction with A680. One way street so cannot approach directly)

Hole in the Wall, Bass
8 Market Street, Colne (on A56, town centre)

Imperial, Thwaites
25 Devonport Road, Blackburn (south of and parallel to Preston New Road, north west of town centre)

Moorgate Arms, Thwaites
Liversey Branch Road, Blackburn (A6062, off A666, south west edge of town)

New Inn, Thwaites
Skipton Old Road, Foulridge (just off and east of A56, north of Colne)

Old England Forever, Matthew Brown
13 Church Street, Clayton-le-Moors (off Wellington Street, off A680, near Junction 7, M75, north of Blackburn)

Old Toll Bar, Thwaites
Accrington Road, Blackburn (A679, eastern outskirts of town, at junction of seven roads)

Ranken Arms, Thwaites
Queen Street, Hoddlesden (small village east of Darwen, off A666)

Red Lion, Taylor
31 Market Street, Colne (on A56, town centre)

Robin Hood, Tetley (Bellhaven Inns)
Holcombe Road, Helmshore (B6235 off B6232 off A56, south of Haslingden)

Strawbury Duck, Hartley/Marston's/Taylor
Hob Lane, Entwistle (OS reference SD 727178. The easiest way is by train to Entwistle Station six miles north of Bolton. By road it is signposted from the Edgworth-Darwen (Roman) Road)

Talbot
Talbot Street, Chipping (OS reference SD 623433, approach from Goosnargh or Longridge)

Uncle Toms Cabin, Thwaites
42 Larkhill Street, Blackburn (just off A666, north of town centre, near the brewery)

In the Thwaites heartland around Blackburn the pubs are fairly homogeneous, often small simple end-terraced properties and many of them relatively unspoilt. In Blackburn the **Imperial**, **Moorgate Arms** and **Uncle Toms Cabin** are good examples. The Imperial is a classic, back street, multi-roomed local. The **Moorgate Arms** is a popular, unpretentious corner pub close to the Leeds-Liverpool Canal. Children are allowed into the small beer garden. Enormous sandwiches offering very good value are available at lunchtimes. **Uncle Toms Cabin** is basic, lively and friendly; a typical East Lancashire urban pub in the shadow of the brewery.

On the outskirts of Blackburn the **Old Toll Bar** is an ancient, stone built pub at a junction of seven roads. It is unusually shaped to fit the site between roads and the three rooms likewise are odd shapes. Despite its age it has not seen too many alterations and it is still a basic, homely local.

A little further up the road in Accrington the **Great Eastern** is an interesting four-roomed back street pub which has recently been smartened up but has retained its character, particularly in the vault, smoke room and tiled lobby. Named after the largest steamship of its day, designed by Brunel in 1856, that may give an indication of its age.

In Darwen, the **Golden Cup** is one of the oldest pubs in the area. It can be identified on an 1834 map on the wall of the pub. Its three small, low-ceilinged rooms are cosy and characterful and there is plenty of space on the cobbled forecourt for sitting out in the good weather.

At Hoddlesden, near Darwen the **Ranken Arms** is a typical village community pub, well cared for, quite unspoilt and catering for diverse activities in its four rooms. There is no juke box or fruit machine but there is a pool table and a piano. It is a popular eating place with an extensive standard menu and daily specials. The pub is named after a local landowning family.

Further East there is a cluster of good interesting pubs in the Colne area, quite near to the **Hole in the Wall**, Foulridge **q.v.** In Colne there is another **Hole in the Wall**, the oldest surviving pub in the town, first mentioned in 1706. Its four rooms with thick stone walls are basic and homely and host to some of the town's characters. Across the road the **Red Lion**, a listed building, is almost as old. It has been opened out a bit but still has character.

Down in the valley, the **Admiral Lord Rodney** is an isolated pub in an area which was once crammed with hillside terraced housing and mills and pubs. It is a vibrant pub which has been changed around a bit but it still retains some remnants of its former 1920s style. The pub is popular for its beer (there is always a guest beer) and its food, (including its infamous mixed grill), served lunchtimes and evenings. It is named after the admiral who defended the West Indies against the French in 1782.

Back at Foulridge another good pub in the vicinity is the **New Inn**, a fairly ordinary pub but with a very pleasant intimate back room. Just over the hill to the West the **Cross Gaits Inn** has a datestone of 1736 together with an inscription 'Good Ale tomorrow for nothing'. It is at an ancient junction of three roads and four trackways and the name is derived from an old word for cross roads. It has been opened up a little inside but there is a small, cosy, beamed snug to the right, off the corridor. There is plenty of room outside on the forecourt and beer garden at the rear. It is a popular eating place, lunchtimes and evenings and it is also popular with walkers. The area is criss-crossed with footpaths and it is not unusual to see a row of boots in the porch.

Another pub which is popular with walkers is the **Strawbury Duck** at Entwistle. It is right by the station and in fact was named the **Station Hotel** until it was given its present idiosyncratic name. The pub has incorporated the 300 year old, next door cottage and there is a warren of small rooms and spaces around a central bar plus an outside drinking area. There are up to three guest beers each week and food, including authentic Indian dishes and vegetarian and fish dishes, is served lunchtimes and evenings and all day Sunday.

If you are visiting the **Victoria**, Great Harwood **q.v.**, it is worth a small detour to experience a wonderful, unspoilt urban pub at Clayton-le-Moors. The **Old England Forever** is a small, four-roomed pub formed out of a couple of stone terraced houses with very little to distinguish it from the adjacent houses apart from the 'Nuttal Lion Ales' windows. It is the only pub left in its original state (outside toilets and all) for miles around out of hundreds which used to look like this. It is quite close to the Leeds-Liverpool Canal.

Another good Lancashire urban pub is the **Foresters** at Haslingden, a lively, noisy, welcoming local. Make for the back room behind the bar with its real coal fire in wintertime. There is nothing special about the building but the pub is a good thriving community local with a lot of games activities spread throughout its three rooms.

A mile or so to the south at Helmshore is the **Robin Hood**, another unspoilt pub in an attractive waterside location adjacent to a mill pond and close to the Helmshore Textile Museum. It is a Victorian pub which has changed very little. There is a nice little snug on the left as you enter. Outside is a small beer garden next to the water which creates a very restful atmosphere. There are a few ducks on the water and the licensee has amassed a collection of over 200 replica ducks of all shapes and sizes adorning all parts of the pub.

Finally, if you visit the picturesque village of Chipping you will find that most of the pubs have been refurbished and taken up-market but the **Talbot** remains a friendly, welcoming and popular place, still intact as a multi-roomed pub and with a good range of facilities and food for visitors.

West Lancashire
and Furness

BLACKPOOL
Ramsden Arms Hotel

204 Talbot Road

On main road between bus and rail stations

Parking in various public car parks nearby

Tetley Bitter; Boddingtons Bitter; Cains Bitter; Hydes Bitter; Jennings Bitter; Ind Coope Burton Ale (there is also a wide selection of malts and blended whiskeys)

The licensee of the **Ramsden Arms** has great pride in the traditional qualities of his pub and the fact that it has won many awards in recent years and appears in many pub guides. It is nominally a Tetley pub, but it has gradually acquired five other popular beers.

As soon as you walk in, it is apparent that this pub is a cut above
the other Blackpool boozers. It dates from 1933 when it replaced
an earlier pub. The whole pub is panelled in oak and decorated
with brass, stags heads and antlers and marquetry panels of fox
hunting scenes. There are basically two rooms but the large
lounge is divided into three separate parlours, each with real coal
fires.

There has been some concession to the Blackpool ethos: the
public bar has become the family room/games room with an
additional (ladies) toilet and television and pool table. There is an
additional pool table in the lounge. Lunchtime food comprises a
selection of starters at around £1, sandwiches, burgers and main
courses such as steak and kidney pie, chicken, scampi, lasagne,
curry, chilli at around £2.25. The pub also offers accommodation
(telephone 0253 23215).

The original name of the pub was the **Golden Lion** and it
belonged to the Thomas Ramsden brewery of Halifax. Ramsdens
were taken over by Allied Breweries in the 1960s.

BLACKPOOL

Saddle

286 Whitegate Drive, Marton

Eastern outskirts, near Stanley Park, A583 near junction with A5073 and B5890

Own car park adjacent to pub

Bass Mild, Special Bitter, Draught Bass; Stones Bitter

The outside of the **Saddle** gives no indication of what you will find inside. It is a small pub with three small rooms plus a bar in one corner and until recently it was like stepping back in time to the First World War. The brewery have carried out some structural changes near the entrances and although they have obviously spent lavishly and introduced some 1990s elements, the interior still has much character and its simplicity has been retained.

The pub is sufficiently far from the centre of Blackpool for it to be mainly a locals pub but it is renowned as a traditional pub with a relaxed, friendly atmosphere, so it does draw customers from further afield plus a few tourists.

There is a smoke room and bar parlour away from the bar and a further room and lobby area next to the bar. All the old fireplaces and wood panelling and mirrors are intact and everything else has been upgraded. There is now some decorative modern floor tiling in the lobby area but it does not look out of place. There is no juke box, no fruit machines and no food. Children are not allowed in the pub but there are tables and benches in the car park.

BOUTH

White Hart

Centre of the village

OS reference SD 328856, north of A590, north of Ulverston between Greenod and Newby Bridge

Street parking and own car park

Boddingtons Bitter; Jennings Bitter; Hartleys XB, Tetley Bitter

The most striking aspect of the **White Hart** is the menagerie of stuffed animals around the place. All the local wildlife is represented plus quite a few outsiders. The thick walls, flag floors and oak beamed ceilings give the authentic lakeland rural atmosphere but it is made comfortable and relaxing by the use of traditional old furniture and settles and two huge log burning fires in wintertime. The pub caters for visitors and locals (it is the only

pub in the village) and there is a separate games room. In summer, you can sit out at the front and absorb the tranquillity of this relatively isolated village, or in the small beer garden at the rear with woodland views.

The pub is reputed to date from the 17th century and is the sole survivor of the many pubs which served the area when there was a thriving charcoal burning industry and when the local port at Greenod used to export wool, slate and copper. Food is served both lunchtimes and early evenings. Children are welcome and there is limited accommodation if you wish to stay (telephone Greenod 0229 861229).

BRINDLE

Cavendish Arms

Sandy Lane

B5256, east of A6, near junction of A6 and M6

Pub has own car park

Burtonwood Mild, Bitter (also 40 brands of malt whiskies are available)

Although this is a very ancient pub, probably as old as the parish church next door, the interior is an 'olde worlde' style created in the 1930s. It seems to have been a very simple village pub before Burtonwood acquired it in 1936 then it was completely refitted with new entrance, new coloured glass windows, solid oak doors and bar fittings, heavy wooden beams and brick fireplaces. Since then an additional room has been brought into the pub and there have been some minor changes all carried out with care and the result is a skilful blend of character and comfort.

The small public bar and three lounge-cum-dining rooms are all furnished in comfortable traditional style and with open coal fires in winter. The pub has always been named after local landowning families, firstly the **Gerrard Arms** and now the **Cavendish Arms**. The coloured glass decoration in the windows depicts the saga of Athelstan, grandson of Alfred the Great, and his battle with the Dane, Anluf in AD 937, which is supposed to have taken place near here. In the public bar there is a stuffed hare, killed in 1875 by the local hunt and preserved to honour its record 37 minute run.

The standard menu is available every lunchtime and evenings, Wednesday to Saturday offering large portions which are good value for money; hot and cold open sandwiches (£3.50 to £3); pies, lasagne, chilli, curry, roast beef £4 to £5; five different fish dishes (around £5) and three vegetarian dishes (£4.50). Well behaved children are welcome at meal times, either in the beer garden or one of the rooms away from the bar. The licensee is a local man who is keen to continue running the pub along traditional lines. It has recently been acquired from the brewery by a pub-owning property group and there are plans to build a restaurant extension on part of the beer garden. The licensee however is keen to ensure that this is handled sensitively. There is no juke box and no electronic machines.

CARTMEL FELL
Masons Arms

Strawberry Bank

South of Windermere, can be approached on various minor roads off the A5074, A592, A590. Look for signs to Cartmel Fell or Bowland Bridge. OS reference SD 413895

Parking in front of the pub

Theakston XB; Lakeland Amazon Bitter, Great Northern, Big Six; plus a regular guest beer plus an impressive range of over 130 foreign bottled beers

The Masons is a renowned pub of character, well known for its exceptional and unusual range of draught and bottled beers and good food (the **Masons Arms** has an entry in the CAMRA Good Pub Food Guide). There are three or four small interconnecting rooms and the combination of low beamed ceilings, uneven slate floors, oak panelled walls and solid old furniture and real fires creates a genuine traditional atmosphere.

The name stems from the time in the 18th century when local Freemasons held secret meetings at the pub. In 1990 the **Masons Arms** began a brewing operation, the Lakeland Brewing Company, producing the three beers listed above plus other occasional brews. A Belgian Kriek-style damson beer is also produced each spring from the pub's own damsons. To complement the excellent choice of beers a regular menu plus daily blackboard menu lists an original and varied selection of meals produced using fresh local produce and featuring local and international dishes all at around £5 to £6. Vegetarians are also well catered for. Food is available lunchtime and evenings. Well behaved children are allowed in the pub at mealtimes.

In good weather you can enjoy your food and drink on the pleasant south facing patio and admire the views over the Winster Valley. On leaving, if you ride or walk on the road south east towards Gummers How viewpoint you will experience some breathtaking views of Lake Windermere. Perhaps the best way to enjoy the hospitality of the **Masons Arms** would be to stay for the night in the self catering accommodation in an adjacent building and not worry about driving home along steep, narrow country lanes (telephone Crossthwaites 04488 486).

CROSTON
Lord Nelson

Out Lane

Just off A581, 6 miles west of Chorley

Pub has own car park

Boddingtons Bitter; Higsons Bitter

One is rather spoilt for choice of good pubs in Croston. The village is sufficiently affluent to sustain its six pubs and, although food catering is an important aspect for many of them, they still function as good traditional village pubs. The **Lord Nelson** probably has a little edge on the others because it manages so well to combine authenticity and tradition with comfort and convenience.

The pub lies just beyond the village green, a solid, farmhouse style of building with thick walls, low ceilings, an old kitchen range and a few reminders of its naval connections – paintings and prints of Nelson's era and a flagpole with a spar which carries, in signal flags, the message 'England expects every man will do his duty'. The four roomed interior is cosy and well furnished and the lighting is just right – not too dim or too bright. In winter there are coal fires and in summer you can sit at tables outside or on the village green. Good quality, home cooked food is served lunchtimes and evenings and children are welcome at mealtimes.

GARSTANG

Royal Oak Hotel

Market Place

Centre of the village

Parking is difficult but there are free public car parks nearby

Robinson's Mild, Best Bitter; Old Tom (in season)

Evening opening 7pm on Mondays, Tuesdays and Wednesdays

The **Royal Oak** is Robinson's most northerly outpost. It is a listed building, part 300 year old and part 500 year old and it occupies a premier position in the town, right by the old cobbled market place. Famous people who have stayed at the **Royal Oak** include Sir Walter Scott and the Victorian novelist William Black. The best time to visit is on market day, Thursday, when it is busy with locals and farmers from round about.

The best part is the oak panelled side room adjacent to the bar. This room looks as though it has not changed for decades and it is usually more crowded than the rest of the pub. Two further rooms are away from the bar, one of them rather too modernised with juke box and fruit machines but it does not interfere with the remainder of the pub. The leaded glazing to the doors, windows

and bar front contain some unusual stained glass motifs including a representation of a glass of beer in the front door. Although the exterior looks badly in need of a refurbishment it would be a pity if the inside were to be altered but apparently this is what is planned by the brewery.

Food is available at lunchtimes. There is a standard menu plus a daily special and the main meals cost around £3. Children are allowed in the rooms away from the bar. The pub also offers accommodation; telephone (0995) 603318 for details.

GREAT URSWICK

General Burgoyne

Centre of the village

OS reference SD 268745, three miles south of Ulverston, approach from A5087 or A590

Parking adjacent

Hartleys XB; Robinson's Bitter;

Not open before 4pm on weekdays; open 12 noon at weekends and there are plans for general lunchtime opening in 1993.

The **General Burgoyne** is renowned as an unspoilt pub of character, hidden away in a part of Cumbria which is generally by-passed by the hordes of lakeland visitors. It did remain unchanged for decades but the current licensees have started to open up other parts of the building as public areas.

The most authentic area is to the left as you enter. It is a long low room, partially divided, with many old black beams and ancient black oak fittings, old wooden settles and an impressive chimney breast and log burning fireplace. One beam has a '1631' date carved into it. The pub has evidently evolved from a farmhouse pub which had its own brewhouse. The brewhouse became the pub's (ground floor) cellar and it is now going to be incorporated into the public areas.

When the work is completed later in 1992 there will be three rooms and a cubby hole downstairs and a function room cum dining room upstairs. If pubs like this have to change then this is a model of how it should be done. It is all being carried out carefully and sensitively, with much thought, using local materials and expertise and in a way which ensures that the pub does not lose touch with its roots in the local community. The pub is used mainly by local people but locals around here come from quite a large catchment area.

Great care is taken with the food also. There are generally 14 main meals available and variations are introduced every few days. The food is freshly cooked each day, there are no chips and the usual price is around £4. Simpler meals of pie and peas and 'tavern broth' are also available, the latter a meal in itself for £1.60. The food is available evenings and lunchtimes when open. Children are able to eat in the pub or in the beer garden with pleasing views of Urswick Tarn.

General Burgoyne was an English general and playwright known as 'Gentleman Johnny' who capitulated to the Americans at Saratoga (1777) in the American War of Independence. In the pub, in an old spice cupboard next to the main fireplace, there is a scull and some say it is Johnny Burgoyne's.

HEATON WITH OXCLIFFE
Golden Ball (Snatchem's)

Mellishaw Lane (left at Nissan Garage)

OS reference SD448616, Overton road, off B5273 Heysham road,off A589 Morecambe Road

Own car park

Mitchell's Dark Mild, Best Bitter, ESB, plus Winter Warmer in season (also some foreign bottled beers)

Despite a rather isolated situation this is a very popular pub because of its position by the River Lune, its historic associations and the fun of knowing that if you stay too long you can be cut off by the tides and have to stay a while longer. It is a very hospitable pub so it would be no real hardship. There are three rooms, tap room, snug and lounge all with real coal fires in winter and a very compact little bar. Outside there is a patio area at the front where you can sit and watch the various water sports on the river and a large beer garden around the back of the pub with a great collection of farm animals to amuse the children. Children are also welcome in the pub in the rooms away from the bar.

It is obviously an old pub, reputed to be 16th century and with its low beamed ceilings, small rooms and oak settles it has a characterful, homely atmosphere. There are quite a few explanations for the nickname **'Snatchems'** but the most plausible is that it was bestowed when Royal Navy press gangs would descend on the pub and snatch a few drunken local fishermen as unwilling recruits.

Food is served lunchtimes and evenings, subject to the tides! and all day Sunday so you can get a drink at anytime on Sunday provided you have a meal. Local fish and seafood is a speciality as you might expect with fresh Lune salmon often available. There is an extensive menu of starters and lunchtime main courses consisting of home made pies, roasts, steaks, chicken, salads and fish plus a range of pizzas. There are also daily blackboard specials and sweets, and sandwiches and snacks. The main course costs around £3 to £4. Evening main courses are more elaborate and rich sauces are a feature. Although the bar is tiny there is a wide selection of drinks and all four sides of the cubby hole are filled with bottles. The wine list offers choices from at least seven different countries.

If you wish to check on the state of the tide the telephone number is (0524) 63317.

HEST BANK

Hest Bank Hotel

2 Hest Bank Lane

Just off A5105 between Morecambe and Carnforth

Own car park

Boddingtons Mild, Bitter plus guest beer

The **Hest Bank** is a thriving and welcoming village pub but its rich historical background gives it added attraction. It was earlier known as the **Sands Inn** when it was on the coaching route across Morecambe Bay sands. The earliest records show it dating from 1554.

The rear portion, built of cobbles and oak beams, is on the lower level of the original road and the pub has gradually expanded, upwards and outwards, over the years. The abbots and monks of Furness Abbey and Cartmel priory would have used the inn; it was occupied by both Cromwellian and Royalist forces during the civil war; it was plundered by Bonnie Prince Charlie's retreating army in 1745 and at times it was the haunt of highwaymen. In 1792 the innkeeper shot and wounded highwayman Edward Crosse. He

was tried and hanged and his body filled with tar and put on a gibbet on the local hanging green where he remained for two years. Coaches such as the Whitehaven Belles and Ulverston Queens would regularly call at the inn bringing many important guests including Prince Frederik of Prussia. The front part of the inn, built in 1799, has, on the top floor, a 'lantern room' where a light was placed to guide the coaches across the sands.

Altogether there are six different rooms and each one has a different floor level. The oldest and lowest part with beamed ceilings and stone mullioned windows is quite evocative of the pub's past and houses a television and dart board. There are two rear rooms, more modern and comfortable, with a bar and two front rooms which act as dining areas, plus a conservatory. Beyond the conservatory is a pleasant beer garden and beyond that a jetty onto the Lancaster Canal which came through here in 1790. You are able to take children into the beer garden, the conservatory and one of the dining rooms.

Customers include locals, canal boaters and ramblers. Food, available lunchtimes and early evenings, consists of wholesome, home cooked soups, roasts, steaks, pies, curries and hot and cold sandwiches plus sweets. A main meal costs around £3 to £4. It is a pub you will want to return to. There are no juke boxes or fruit machines.

HEYSHAM

Royal Hotel

7 Main Street, Lower Heysham

Turn off the A5105 towards the sea. Main Street is off the main square in the centre of Heysham village

Public car park adjacent to main square

Mitchell's Dark Mild, Best Bitter

The **Royal** is a listed building, part of a terrace of former farmhouse and barn and stables. Reputedly a smugglers pub at one time, it is known to date back to the early 16th century. It is in a very narrow street in the oldest part of the town. As with many old pubs it has an idiosyncratic layout. As you enter, to the left, there are two fairly plain, wood panelled rooms, the furthest of which has a pool table and free standing juke box and an old

kitchen range. Children are allowed into these two rooms until 7.30 pm. To the right there is a delightful cosy little snug with a bar and real fire. In the centre of the building there is a lobby area from the rear entrance and through here is the main lounge, a large room with low beamed ceiling, another real fire and furnished with oak settles and traditional furniture and decorations. At the rear of the pub there is a pleasant walled beer garden with dove cotes.

Food is available at lunchtimes and comprises anything with chips, plus toasties, burgers, ploughmans and salads. The most expensive item is £3.25 and most meals cost around £2.50 to £3. Heysham Sands is just a little further along Main Street.

NEAR SAWREY

Tower Bank Arms

Southern outskirts of village on B5285 which can be approached from Ambleside and Hawkshead in the north or by the ferry across Lake Windermere to the east, OS reference SD 370956

Forecourt parking and a small area on opposite side of the road

Theakston Best Bitter, XB, Old Peculiar; Matthew Brown Mild; Younger Scotch Bitter

The main attraction for most people in this picturesque part of the Lake District is Hill Top Farm, the home of Beatrix Potter, the Victorian children's author. It is the most visited house in the Lake District but the pub is also an attraction in its own right. It is apparently still recognisable from an illustration in 'The Tale of

Jemima Puddleduck'. If you want to avoid the Beatrix Potter crowds, visit out of season.

The National Trust owns Hill Top Farm and, to prevent undue commercial exploitation of the literary connections, they also acquired the pub in 1976. The Trust owns 40 pubs altogether throughout the country and is an excellent steward of our pub heritage, exercising strict controls on alterations or decorations which could be out of character with a building or its environment.

The pub is run in a relaxed and hospitable way with a good range of beers at reasonable prices for the area. Some of the more attractive features are the intimate little window seats in the bay window, the stone flagged floors, the old wood burning kitchen range which provides a wonderful warmth in winter and the high settle back benches and other traditional furniture. There is an additional room at the rear which acts as a family room and main dining area.

The pub features in the CAMRA Good Pub Food Guide and the food is of high quality and variety including daily specials such as venison pie, chicken breast stuffed with leek and stilton and smoked salmon platter at £4 to £6. There are also many standard dishes at £3 to £4. The **Tower Bank Arms** also provides accommodation so if you are planning to stay in the area you could do worse than stay here (telephone Hawkshead 09666 334).

OVERTON

Ship Hotel

9 Main Street

Overton is signed from the B5273 south of Morecambe or from Heysham

Car park adjacent to pub

Thwaites Best Mild, Bitter

Evening opening time is 7pm

The **Ship** is probably Lancashire's closest approximation to George Orwell's mythical perfect pub, the 'Moon Under Water', a Victorian pub rich in that indefinable quality of atmosphere and other essential ingredients: some locals, unpretentious food, pub games and outside facilities for the summer.

The **Ship** is a genuine late Victorian village pub which has been remarkably well preserved so that you feel you are stepping back in time. The vault is rather spartan though it has a piano and there is now a pool room at the rear in what was probably part of the private quarters at one time but the rest of the pub – the lobby area, the lounge, the cosy snug – look unchanged for generations. The polished wooden bar fittings are original Victorian and there are various antiques around the pub including an intriguing mounted collection of stuffed birds and birds eggs. There are a couple of original fireplaces also with real coal fires in winter. The pub was known as 'Ma Macluskie's' until recently when Ma Macluskie retired after a 50 year reign. In those days the pub belonged to a local Lancaster brewer Yates and Jackson.

For some obscure reason the pub is not a listed building but the original brewhouse is. The brewhouse was the last resting place of Sambo, the black servant of a local merchant, who pined away and died in 1736 and his headstone can be seen at nearby

Sunderland Point. The pub is unpretentious and slightly shabby but clean and comfortable. There is no intrusive juke box. Plain, home cooked food and thick sandwiches are available at lunchtimes-cooked food Wednesday to Sunday only and children are welcome.

PRESTON

Black Horse Hotel

166 Friargate

Pedestrianised area near the market

Hartleys XB; Robinson's Mild, Bitter, Best Bitter, Old Tom

Closed Sunday lunchtimes and 4pm to 7.30pm on Saturdays

This gem of a pub is well appreciated and well used by local people. The interior is architecturally splendid and slightly distressed like a good antique should be. It is comparable to the **Prince Arthur** in Liverpool – a masterpiece but with no airs and graces. The pub was built by Kays Atlas Brewery of Manchester in 1898 and is one of only two remaining Kay's pubs. The brewery was taken over by Robinsons in the 1930s.

The **Black Horse** stands on a prominent corner position in a busy shop-

ping area and dispenses a good range of beers and cheap meals to a wide cross section of customers. The building is an odd shape and so are the rooms. The vault is a riot of decorative detail from the ornate, bow fronted, tiled bar to the mosaic floor, ribbed plaster ceiling and leaded and coloured glass screens and windows. The tiny back parlour is unique – a three sided recess with bench seating and room for a couple of tables and with walls of stained glass and mirror. There are also two cosy side rooms with open fires in winter and a drinking passage between the mahogany bar fittings and the stairs. Upstairs is a function room with a bar.

The pub is a listed building due to the efforts of the local CAMRA branch to gain recognition for its qualities. The listing description comments on its 'remarkably unaltered interior of the period'. Juke box music usually pervades the pub. Food is available at lunch times and the meals are very good value at £1.50 or £2 for the daily special.

ULVERSTON

Rose and Crown

King Street

Near the market and the rear entrance can be accessed from the main car park off the market square

Hartleys XB; Robinson's Best Bitter, Mild

The best time to visit this pub is on a cold winter evening, early enough to take a seat in the small snug on the right as you enter. It looks as though it has hardly been altered for decades. It can only seat about a dozen people and the main feature is the enormous log fire in a dog grate which is about knee height so it throws its heat throughout the room. There is a stone flagged floor, wood panelled ceiling and the room is furnished with comfortable settle back seats. The remainder of the pub has been refurbished

somewhat but retains some flagged floor and the occasional exposed beam.

The pub is very popular for its food, served lunchtimes and evenings. There is a prominent, permanent menu board outside with prices displayed so that you know exactly what to expect – very commendable – and specials of the day on a blackboard inside. There is a good choice of vegetarian dishes. Most meals are about £3.50 and sweets are available at £1.50. A cobbled back yard becomes a pleasant sitting out area in summer. The piped music is not too loud but the live music on Wednesday evenings often is. On market days, Thursdays and Saturdays, Ulverston pubs are much busier and many remain open all day.

SOME FURTHER SUGGESTIONS

Bispham Hotel, Samuel Smith
70 Red Bank Road, Bispham, Blackpool (A584, 200 yards from the Promenade)

Black Bull, Greenalls
Hall Lane, Mawdesley(OS reference SD 500152,west of Chorley,best approached from B5246 or B5250)

Black Horse, Freehouse with a good selection of beers
Westland Road, Croston (A581, 6 miles west of Chorley)

Burn Naze, Tetley plus guest beers
1 Gamble Road, Thornton (6 miles north of Blackpool centre, just off B5268, next to ICI works)

Coach and Horses, Boddingtons
Preston Old Road, Freckleton (A584, midway between Blackpool and Preston)

Crown, Mitchell's/Tetley/Thwaites
Station Road, Croston (near BR station, off A581, 6 miles west of Chorley)

Eagle and Child, Freehouse with a good range of beers
Church Road, Wharles (OS reference SD 448356, between Preston and Blackpool. Approach off A583 at Kirkham or off B5269 at Inskip).

Empress Hotel, Thwaites
59 Exchange Street, Blackpool (behind BR station, off Pleasant Street)

Fleece, Mitchell's
Dolphinholme (situated at crossroads just outside the village, $1\frac{1}{2}$ miles east of Junction 33, M6)

Fleetwood Arms, Boddingtons/Higsons
188 Dock street, Fleetwood (just off A585 towards the docks)

George Hotel, Thwaites
89 Church Street, Preston (eastern part of town centre, within one way system)

Kings Arms, Hartleys/Robinson's
Quarry Brow, Barrow (north of town centre, approach from Gill Lane or Dalton Lane)

Kings Arms, Whitbread
The Square, Cartmel (centre of town, 2 miles from Grange-over-Sands, 3 miles from A590)

Market Tavern, Theakston/Younger
21 Cleveland Street, Chorley (centre of town, adjacent to market)

Moorlands, Mitchell's
Quarry Road, Lancaster (south east of town centre)

Old Blue Bell, Samuel Smith
114 Church Street, Preston (eastern part of town centre, within one way system)

Ship, Hartleys/Robinson's
Bowmanstead, Coniston (half mile south of Coniston, just off A593; sharp steep turning)

Three Mariners, Mitchells
Bridge Lane, Lancaster (just off one way system, below the castle, opposite the bus station)

White Bull, Matthew Brown/Theakston/Younger
Garstang Road, Bilsborrow (A6, 7 miles north of Preston)

Yates Wine Lodge, Thwaites
Market Street, Chorley (A6, town centre)

Pubs in the Furness area, traditionally 'Lancashire-over-the-Sands', are an integral part of the tourist industry there and are generally very hospitable to visitors. In addition to the five pubs of renown listed as main entries, there are a further three which should be mentioned.

At Cartmel, the remains of the ancient priory and the local racecourse are the main attractions. The **Kings Arms**, in the main square, is a very civilised pub with a relaxed atmosphere. Food is available at most times including afternoon tea. There are three separate areas including a dining room at the rear and there is plenty of seating on the cobbled forecourt. The standard menu and the daily specials offer good quality food at around £5 for a main dish.

The **Ship** at Coniston is a small, out of the way pub which provides an extensive range of facilities for visitors and a convivial atmosphere. The footpath to Seathwaite and Dunnerdale goes right past the front door so it attracts many walkers. The food is of sufficient quality and originality for the pub to feature in the CAMRA Good Pub Food Guide. The blackboard lists of daily specials are often quite elaborate dishes which you would not expect to find in a little roadside pub like this.

If you visit Barrow it is best to avoid the town centre pubs and make for the **Kings Arms** on the northern outskirts. It is about the last traditional pub left in the area with two small restful rooms furnished in a homely way and no juke box or fruit machines.

Moving south to the historic city of Lancaster, seek out two worthy Mitchells pubs: the **Moorlands** and the **Three Mariners**. The **Moorlands** is a large, multi-roomed locals pub dating from the turn of the century, which has retained some original features. The **Three Mariners** is said to date from the 17th century and is probably the oldest pub in Lancaster. It is partially built into the rock below Lancaster Castle and the beer cellar is actually carved out of the rock face at a level higher than the bar. There are mullioned windows and old oak beams and columns in the two small rooms. It used to be known as the **Carpenters Arms** but reverted to its original name a few years ago.

At Dolphinholme, just south of Lancaster, there is another good Mitchells pub, the **Fleece**. It is a former farmhouse and coaching inn dating from 1797 with three rooms of character, low, oak beamed ceilings and open fires.

Continuing south we arrive at the **White Bull** at Bilsborrow. it is a friendly and unspoilt two-roomed pub with real coal fires in winter. In summer you can sit by the Lancaster Canal which runs right behind the pub.

When in Blackpool you might expect to come across some quite vulgar sights. If you take a look in the **Bispham Hotel** your expectations will be fulfilled but it works well as a Blackpool pub. it is a recently revamped 1930s building with some attractive coloured glass windows, a few garish statues and a large stage for live floor shows.

The **Empress** is a much modernised pub but it has retained its separate rooms including an enormous public bar with a full size snooker table. It was built 1847 and many celebrities from the worlds of politics and entertainment have stayed at the pub. It has managed to appear in every issue of the Good Beer Guide. The pub is near to but not part of the main tourist areas and it provides a friendly welcome and serves good value food in the holiday season.

On the northern outskirts of Blackpool the **Burn Naze** fulfils a useful function as a basic but comfortable community pub with a public bar in a part of Lancashire where most pubs have gone upmarket and a great many are more like restaurants than pubs. It has four rooms altogether. Not much of the original interior has survived. The pub is very sports and games oriented and there is often live music.

Just a little further up the road at Fleetwood the **Fleetwood Arms** is another good, basic pub, a three-roomed, dockside tavern, unspoilt and characterful and frequented by some of the few remaining trawlermen and local characters.

South of Blackpool at Freckleton, the **Coach and Horses** comes into the same category as a fairly plain but comfortable traditional village pub with three rooms.

In the same area the **Eagle and Child** at Wharles is worth seeking out in its isolated spot. It is a cosy, thatch roofed, country inn whose main attractions are the excellent beers and collection of antique furniture and fireplaces. No food is served, children are not allowed, there is no beer garden and they do not open weekday lunchtimes.

At Preston a visit to the **Black Horse** q.v. is a must and then have a look at the **George** which is a listed, mid 19th century pub, basic and with an unaltered layout of four rooms, probably the last remaining interior of its kind in the Preston area.

A few doors away, the **Old Blue Bell** is another listed building, 18th century with the remains of its original brewhouse at the rear. There is one large lounge and two small snugs all fitted out in solid, good quality Sam Smith style.

In Chorley, the **Market Tavern** was until recently a Walker's pub and its four tiny rooms were cosy, atmospheric and full of character. In fact it recently won a CAMRA 'Pub of the Year' award in recognition of its qualities. However, when the lease on the building expired recently, it was taken over by a local pub owning group and it is now a rather bizarre experience to drink there because, while the fabric of the pub has not changed, everything else has-the beers, the bar service and the customers. But it is still worth popping in as long as you do not mind loud rave music.

Still in Chorley, there is the last of the old spit and sawdust style **Yates Wine Lodge**, a cavernous room with bare, scrubbed boards and simple furniture arranged around the edges. The first Wine Lodge was in Oldham in 1884 and from there they spread throughout Lancashire and principal cities all over the country. All the remaining Lodges have been changed out of recognition through refurbishment except the Chorley site. It was previously the **George Inn** and was acquired by the Yates Brothers in 1905.

Croston is due west of Chorley. It is a pretty village and in addition to the **Lord Nelson** q.v., the **Black Horse** and the **Crown** can be recommended. The **Black Horse** sets out to provide full facilities and a high level of service for all comers. They are renowned for their beer range and mini beer festivals, managing to put on 240 different beers each year. Not surprisingly it has won many awards from CAMRA. Food is available lunchtime and evening.

The **Crown** is an unusual pub with a rather quirky layout. It is much larger than it looks from the outside and has a central bar serving six separate areas. It serves generous portions of home cooked food at reasonable prices.

Last but not least, the **Black Bull** at Mawdesley is a 400 year old stone building in attractive rural surroundings. It has a beer garden, two plush lounges and a tap room full of character with ancient wooden doors and a black leaded range equiped with an enourmous poker. Well prepared, home cooked food is available lunchtimes and evenings.

Geographical Index

The Section Numbers indicate the area of the old county:

1. Manchester Area
2. Liverpool and South Lancashire Area
3. Ribble, Calder, Pendle Area
4. West Lancashire and Furness Area

The main pub entries are in **bold type**, and the remainder are further suggestions of pubs worth visiting.

Town	Pub Name	Section
Blacko	Cross Gaits Inn	3
Blackpool	Bispham Hotel	4
	Empress Hotel	
	Ramsden Arms Hotel	
	Saddle	
Bolton	**Howcroft**	1
	Kings Head	
	Sweet Green Tavern	
	Ye Olde Man and Scythe	
Bootle	Railway	2
Bouth	**White Hart**	4
Brierfield	**Waggon and Horses**	3
Brindle	**Cavendish Arms**	4
Burnley	**Swan Inn**	3
Bury	**White Lion**	1
Cartmel	Kings Arms	4
Cartmel Fell	**Masons Arms**	4
Cheetham, Manchester	Queens Arms	1
Chipping	Talbot	3
Chorley	Market Tavern	4
	Yates Wine Lodge	
Chorlton-cum-Hardy, Manchester	**Beech**	1
Chorlton-on-Medlock, Manchester	Kings Arms Hotel	1
	Mawson Hotel	
Clayton-le-Moors	Old England Forever	3
Clitheroe	**New Inn**	3
Collyhurst, Manchester	Marble Arch	1
Colne	Admiral Lord Rodney	3
	Hole in the Wall	
	Red Lion	
Coniston	Ship	4
Crosby	Crows Nest	2
Croston	Black Horse	4
	Crown	
	Lord Nelson	
Darwen	Golden Cup	3
Denton	**Red Lion Hotel**	1
Didsbury	**Royal Oak**	1

Town	*Pub Name*	*Section*
Longridge	**Towneley Arms**	3
Liverpool City Centre	Beehive	2
	Globe	2
	Lion Tavern	
	Oxford	
	Philharmonic	
	Pig and Whistle	
	Poste House	
	Roscoe Head	
	Vines	
	White Star	
	Ye Cracke	
	Ye Hole in ye Wall	
Lydiate	Running Horses	2
	Scotch Piper	
Manchester City Centre	Beerhouse	1
	Briton's Protection	
	Castle Hotel	
	Circus Tavern	
	Hare and Hounds	
	Mr. Thomas's Chop House	
	Peveril of the Peak	
	Sinclair's Oyster Bar	
	Unicorn Hotel	
Mawdesley	Black Bull	4
Middleton	**Old Boars Head**	1
	Tandle Hill Tavern	
Mossley	**Colliers Arms**	1
Near Sawrey	**Tower Bank Arms**	4
Oldham	**Gardeners Arms**	1
	Royal Oak	
	Royal Oak	
Openshaw	Concert	1
	Oddfellows Arms	
	Smithfield	
	Wrexham	
Ormskirk	**Buck i' th' Vine Inn**	2
	Greyhound	

Sample the delights of country pubs, and enjoy some of the finest walks with our expanding range of 'real ale' books:

PUB WALKS IN THE PEAK DISTRICT
– Les Lumsdon and Martin Smith

MORE PUB WALKS IN THE PEAK DISTRICT –
Les Lumsdon and Martin Smith

PUB WALKS IN LANCASHIRE – Neil Coates

PUB WALKS IN THE PENNINES
– Les Lumsdon and Colin Speakman

PUB WALKS IN THE LAKE DISTRICT – Neil Coates

PUB WALKS IN THE YORKSHIRE DALES – Clive Price

PUB WALKS IN THE COTSWOLDS – Laurence Main

HEREFORDSHIRE WALKS – REAL ALE AND CIDER COUNTRY
– Les Lumsdon

PUB WALKS IN CHESHIRE – Jen Darling

– all 'Pub Walks' books are just £6.95 each

There are even more books for outdoor people in our catalogue, including:

EAST CHESHIRE WALKS – Graham Beech

WEST CHESHIRE WALKS – Jen Darling

WEST PENNINE WALKS – Mike Cresswell

RAMBLES AROUND MANCHESTER – Mike Cresswell

WELSH WALKS: Dolgellau and the Cambrian Coast
– Laurence Main and Morag Perrott

WELSH WALKS: Aberystwyth and District
– Laurence Main and Morag Perrott

OFF-BEAT CYCLING IN THE PEAK DISTRICT – Clive Smith (£6.95)

THE GREATER MANCHESTER BOUNDARY WALK –
Graham Phythian

THE THIRLMERE WAY – Tim Cappelli (£6.95)

THE MARCHES WAY – Les Lumsdon (£6.95)

– all £5.95 except where indicated

We also publish:

Guidebooks for local towns

Spooky stories, myths and legends

Manchester City and Manchester United popular histories

and, under our Sigma Press banner, over 100 computer books!

All of our books are available from your local bookshop.

In case of difficulty, or to obtain our complete catalogue, please contact:

**Sigma Leisure,
1 South Oak Lane,
Wilmslow, Cheshire SK9 6AR**

Phone: 0625 - 531035 Fax: 0625 - 536800

ACCESS and VISA orders welcome – call our friendly sales staff or use our 24 hour Answerphone service!

Most orders are despatched on the day we receive your order – you could be enjoying our books in just a couple of days.

NEW AUTHORS WELCOME!

Sigma Leisure like to hear from authors with interesting ideas for new books. Contact Graham Beech, the commissioning editor, for an informal chat.